LOVERS AND EXECUTIONERS

by
JOHN STRAND

A comedy based on the play
La Femme juge et partie (1669)
by
Antoine Jacob, known as Montfleury (1640-85)

Dramatic Publishing
Woodstock, Illinois • London, England • Melbourne, Australia

*** NOTICE ***

The amateur and stock acting rights to this work are controlled exclusively by THE DRAMATIC PUBLISHING COMPANY without whose permission in writing no performance of it may be given. Royalty fees are given in our current catalog and are subject to change without notice. Royalty must be paid every time a play is performed whether or not it is presented for profit and whether or not admission is charged. A play is performed any time it is acted before an audience. All inquiries concerning amateur and stock rights should be addressed to:

DRAMATIC PUBLISHING
P. O. Box 129, Woodstock, Illinois 60098

COPYRIGHT LAW GIVES THE AUTHOR OR THE AUTHOR'S AGENT *THE EXCLUSIVE RIGHT TO MAKE COPIES.* This law provides authors with a fair return for their creative efforts. Authors earn their living from the royalties they receive from book sales and from the performance of their work. Conscientious observance of copyright law is not only ethical, it encourages authors to continue their creative work. This work is fully protected by copyright. No alterations, deletions or substitutions may be made in the work without the prior written consent of the publisher. No part of this work may be reproduced or transmitted in any form or by any means, electronic or mechanical, including photocopy, recording, videotape, film, or any information storage and retrieval system, without permission in writing from the publisher. It may not be performed either by professionals or amateurs without payment of royalty. All rights, including but not limited to the professional, motion picture, radio, television, videotape, foreign language, tabloid, recitation, lecturing, publication, and reading are reserved.

For performance of any songs and recordings mentioned in this play which are in copyright, the permission of the copyright owners must be obtained or other songs and recordings in the public domain substituted.

©MCMXCIX by
JOHN STRAND

Printed in the United States of America
All Rights Reserved
(LOVERS AND EXECUTIONERS)

ISBN 0-87129-910-0

IMPORTANT BILLING AND CREDIT REQUIREMENTS

All producers of the Play *must* give credit to the Author(s) of the Play in all programs distributed in connection with performances of the Play and in all instances in which the title of the Play appears for purposes of advertising, publicizing or otherwise exploiting the Play and/or a production. The name of the Author(s) *must* also appear on a separate line, on which no other name appears, immediately following the title, and *must* appear in size of type not less than fifty percent the size of the title type. *On all programs this notice must appear:*

"Produced by special arrangement with
THE DRAMATIC PUBLISHING COMPANY of Woodstock, Illinois"

All producers of LOVERS AND EXECUTIONERS must include the following acknowledgment on the title page of all programs distributed in connection with performances of the play and on all advertising and promotional materials:

"Originally commissioned and produced by Arena Stage,
Washington, D.C., March 1998."

Lovers and Executioners is a translation and free adaptation of the 17th-century French comedy, *La Femme juge et partie* (Literally: "The Wife, Judge and Accuser") (1669) by Antoine Jacob de Montfleury.

Antoine Jacob, known as Montfleury (1640-85), was a contemporary of Molière, and one of his many bitter enemies. Antoine's father, Zacharie Jacob, also known as Montfleury (1600-67), was a playwright and renowned actor with the Hotel de Bourgogne, a rival theater troupe in Paris. Montfleury senior gained some infamy among later historians when (according to the playwright Racine) he denounced Molière to the king, accusing the greater playwright of having married his own daughter, a rumor that plagued Molière throughout his later years. Molière had attacked Montfleury publicly in his play *The Impromptu of Versailles*, mocking the rotund actor's playing style. In retaliation, Montfleury junior, a playwright, wrote *The Impromptu of the Hotel de Condé*, in which Molière was attacked in similar fashion.

Both Montfleurys wrote plays, although the son's are superior. His plays were highly regarded during his day, and some were considered by his contemporaries to rival those of Molière. *La Femme juge et partie*, considered his masterpiece, was performed nearly 500 times at the Comedie-Française through the mid-19th century; a comic opera was made of it in the 1860s. No version of the play has been performed, before now, in the United States.

Lovers and Executioners, however, is a new and quite different version, heavily adapted. Following a convention of the period, I have borrowed only a portion of the plot outline, the names of the characters and certain conventions of the genre. All else is new invention. Even so, the present version qualifies as something of a resurrection of the unjustly forgotten Antoine Jacob de Montfleury.

— John Strand

For Amanda

This translation and free adaptation of *Lovers and Executioners* was commissioned by Arena Stage, Washington, D.C. It premiered on the Fichandler Stage at Arena on February 27, 1998, directed by Kyle Donnelly and included the following artists:

CAST

Bernard	JAMES WARWICK
Julie/Frederic	JUDITH HAWKING
Constance	ELLEN KARAS
Don Lope	J. FRED SHIFFMAN
Guzman	WESLEY MANN
Octavius	T J EDWARDS
Beatrice	NANCY ROBINETTE

PRODUCTION STAFF

Settings	ZACK BROWN
Costumes	LINDSAY W. DAVIS
Lighting	NANCY SCHERTLER
Sound	ROB MILBURN
Fight Choreographer	DAVID DEBESSE
Voice and Speech Consultant	SARAH FELDER
Dramaturg	MARY RESING
Technical Director	JAMES GLENDINNING
Stage Manager	BARBARA ROLLINS
Director of Production	GUY BERGQUIST
Assistant Stage Manager	SARAH M. DELIA
Stage Management Fellow	ANJALI BIDANI
Directing Intern	BLAKE A LAWRENCE
Assistant Fight Choreographer	BRAD WALLER
Fight Captain	T J EDWARDS

LOVERS AND EXECUTIONERS

A play in 5 short acts
For 4 men and 3 women

CHARACTERS

BERNARD .... wealthy bourgeois, 40+
JULIE .... his wife, 30s;
                      she also appears disguised as FREDERIC
CONSTANCE................ pursued by Bernard, 20s
DON LOPE....... Spanish captain, in love with Constance
GUZMAN.......................... valet to Bernard
OCTAVIUS........................... valet to Julie
BEATRICE............ servant/companion to Constance

PLACE:
The principle action takes place in a town outside Paris.

TIME:
The mid-1660s.

Single set/two locations
Running time: Two hours

ACT ONE

SCENE ONE

(A ship at sea. The sound of wind and waves: a storm is rising. BERNARD is at the rail. His valet GUZMAN, pacing nervously, is watching something in the distance, across the ship in the opposite direction.)

BERNARD
The sea runs against us. The wind is all wrong.
Can this vessel sail no faster? What is taking so long?
The storm is rising. The sky in anger grows black
And conspires with the waves to prepare its attack.
Where is the wind?

GUZMAN
The wind? In the sky, Sir.

BERNARD
Fool! What direction?

GUZMAN
North by south?

BERNARD
Do you spy her?
Damn your eyes, if you do. Give me open sea.
Put deep, dark water between this isle and me.

Curse this drunken crew! Must they move so slow?
Can she still be seen? Answer!

GUZMAN

Sir, even so.
On the shore where you left her, there she stays.

BERNARD

I left her? Not I.

GUZMAN

Look. Now she prays.

BERNARD

She did this to herself. This action I abhor.
Her own deceit has brought her to this shore.

GUZMAN

She'll be frightened, near to death. Crippled with fear.
Master, you have won. Let her torture stop here.

BERNARD

Shut up.

GUZMAN

One word from you, and she is reprieved.
Go back and reclaim her. Sir, by your leave—

(BERNARD looks back; for a moment, his resolve weakens.)

BERNARD

Go back...?

GUZMAN

I give the order myself, if you wish.

BERNARD
Shut up, I say, or I'll throw you to the fish!
Where's your stomach, coward? I'm within my rights.

GUZMAN
Or it's murder, if not. That's a damnable sight,
A woman left to die on a deserted shore.

BERNARD
Justice, not murder! I shall hear no more!
Vengeance is my duty. It was lawful and just.
She dishonored me. I have done what I must.

GUZMAN
To your mercy, the crew appeal. They fear a curse.
The captain himself, Sir, returns your purse,
And begs you take pity—

BERNARD
Let him keep his reward!
I purchased his silence. He swore on his sword.
Sail on, you cowards! Bring this misery to an end,
Before the sea swallows all and claims its revenge.
The wind grows mad. Like a ghost, it moans.
Ghosts, they say, fear water. She can't follow us home.

GUZMAN *(staring off).*
There, Sir! Look there. She's freed her hands.

BERNARD
To look on her now would blind me.

GUZMAN
Now she stands,
And cries out.

BERNARD
Stop up my ears!

GUZMAN
A curse on this crime.

BERNARD
Hell itself did fashion this place and time!
(To the winds.) Damn my soul! What have I done!?

(JULIE, on the shore in the distance, kneels in the sand and calls out to the departing ship.)

JULIE
What have I done? Husband!

JULIE & BERNARD
What have I done!?

(Rising sound of the wind and the waves. Lights fade to black.)

SCENE TWO

(A town outside Paris. The central square, with a fountain. Enter running and laughing, BEATRICE, a maidservant.)

BEATRICE

Enough! Enough of your games. I refuse to play.
You keep your distance. What will people say?
(She halts. She looks behind, then all around, expecting to see her pursuer, but there is no one in evidence.)
Chasing me like a schoolboy through the town square.
It's disrespectful, I tell you. Guzman? Are you there?
Are you hiding? You come out here, I demand it.
Guzman? This is not funny. Guzman, dammit!
One last chance. I mean it. Stop this masquerade!

(GUZMAN, meanwhile, has crept up silently behind her.)

GUZMAN

Beatrice!

BEATRICE

Oh! You monster—!

GUZMAN

Pretty little maid...

BEATRICE

That was cruel. You nearly frightened me to death.

GUZMAN

You're delicious, my sweet, when you're all out of breath.

(Business: He places his hand on her breast; she slaps his cheek. He places the other hand on the other breast; she slaps the other cheek; etc. He fakes one; she stops in mid-slap. Again, his hand; she slaps, he ducks, etc.)

BEATRICE
Will you stop, you great fool? And tell me the news.
In detail. *(Grandly:)* Or henceforth your kisses I refuse.

GUZMAN
The news? Heaven's full of thunder, rivers full of rain.
The earth is full of dirt. And master's gone insane.

BEATRICE
Bernard? Insane?

GUZMAN
Completely.

BEATRICE
And why?

GUZMAN
Such evidence as only a woman could deny.

BEATRICE
He wants to remarry. Does that make him mad?

GUZMAN
It'll never make him rich, but sooner make him sad.

BEATRICE
He's rich enough now. Richer than most

Men of this town. Bernard can boast
Of property and gold, the respect of his peers.

GUZMAN
She'll piss it all away for him within the year.

BEATRICE
How so? Some logic, sweet dunce, to defend you.
Give me reasons.

GUZMAN
Oh, I intend to.
Bernard, being charged with burden, for life—

BEATRICE
What burden?

GUZMAN
The most burdensome: a wife.
Yet by heaven, was pardoned.

BEATRICE
Oh?

GUZMAN
And a widower made.
A gift that husbands each and every day
Beg to receive. Was he the wiser for it?
No. And he will live to deplore it.
After three years of freedom, again the crime.
He will take himself a wife, for a second time!
Newer. Younger. Heavier a load. You call that sane?

BEATRICE
I do.

GUZMAN
Not "I do"! A curse on that refrain!

BEATRICE
My Constance, I admit, is yet young and naive.

GUZMAN
She is a lethal flirt.

BEATRICE
She does like to tease.
But it's pleasing to love, and a marriage is sweet
When it is well made.

GUZMAN
But would you leap,
Once burned, into the very flames
That scorched you? Do you call that sane?

BEATRICE
It would seem mad to you, who leap into beds,
Leaving but promises and stealing maiden heads.

GUZMAN
Sweet Bea. Honestly given, and humbly received.
Though I have oft entertained, I've never deceived.
I am straight.

BEATRICE.
Too frequent, straight up.

GUZMAN
A touch of lust.
But healthily, Bea! Do believe me.

BEATRICE
I must.

GUZMAN
If this new wife plays Bernard as rudely as the first...

BEATRICE
Let Julie rest in peace. I'll not hear her cursed.
I cried a month through when I learned she was gone.
Two years I served Julie, before Constance took me on.
She was virtue and innocence, purity and light.

GUZMAN
Virtue, you call it? You were present that night
When the husband got his horns.

BEATRICE
Not so.

GUZMAN
Bernard, unsuspecting, arrived late to home.
So not to wake Julie, silently he crept
To the door—when out from its shadow leapt
A strange man. Master gave chase.
The intruder disappeared without a trace.
Bernard, raging mad, returned to find you,
Who, seeing nothing, could give him no clue.
He grabbed you by the throat—

BEATRICE
Marks I still bear—

GUZMAN
And threatened to kill you if you did not swear
The truth: her lover it was who fled that night.

BEATRICE
No more. The memory fills me with fright.
He swore me to silence, by the blade of his knife.
If he lost his reputation, I would lose my life.

GUZMAN
"Reputation"? Such hypocrisy I cannot abide.
Ah, those who have most have the most to hide.
A monument he erects to his wife, dear departed.
A monument to himself, the broken-hearted
Widower, tragic Bernard. If this town only knew.
There's a secret here, Bea, and a dark one, too.

BEATRICE
Deliver me from secrets. To the keeper, they're a plague.

GUZMAN
It's by deception and secrets that the great are made,
And also undone. Dearest Bea: shall I tell?

BEATRICE
Knowing is trouble...

> GUZMAN *(bowing, as if to leave)*.
> Your servant.

BEATRICE
>   But not knowing is hell.

GUZMAN
Your Julie, it seems, had her secret vice.

BEATRICE
Did she?

GUZMAN
And Bernard, learning of it, extracted the price.

BEATRICE
Tell me. He whipped her?

GUZMAN
Whipping's too mild.

BEATRICE
Bound her? And starved her?

GUZMAN
Fit for a child.
No, the cuckold was silent and smiling, composed.
While in his dark heart, it was murder he chose.
Vowing travel and rest, he took her to sea.
But her return voyage was never to be.

BEATRICE
I begged to go with her, but I was forbidden.

GUZMAN
With reason. Bernard kept his stratagem hidden.
Without warning, nor pity, nor even good-bye,
Upon a small island, he left Julie to die.

BEATRICE
No! She died at sea—of some foul disease!

GUZMAN
So all were told—and so you believed.

BEATRICE
Murderer!

GUZMAN
Who knew his duty. Harsh, to be sure.
He took his revenge. Now his honor's secure.

BEATRICE
Honorable assassin!

GUZMAN
His action was lawful.

BEATRICE
If you knew, if you knew—! The truth is too awful!

GUZMAN *(looking off)*.
Your mistress. Not a word must you breathe
Of the story I told you. Quick. Take your leave.

(Exit swiftly BEATRICE. Enter CONSTANCE, in full flirt, accompanied by FREDERIC. They cross, regally. GUZMAN bows, exaggeratedly. They exit; GUZMAN remains. After a beat, enter BERNARD, reflective, a bit morose.)

SCENE THREE

BERNARD
To our own simple joy, Guzman, we are enemy.
Man does ever craft his own misery.

GUZMAN
Dunno, Sir. There's a good dozen working on mine.

BERNARD
To let fortune slip away—there's the basest crime.

GUZMAN
Master, what is this? A cloud of cares upon your head,
You who are soon to be so joyously wed?
Marriage brings a state, Sir, of— Of marital bliss,
And joy and, and... Joy. So, Sir: What is this?

BERNARD
Interminable night. Again, I've not slept.
Herbs and potions have no effect
On my dreams. More vivid they grow
With time, until even by day I scarcely know,
Were they real? I felt upon my neck
The icy grip of one in robes, who did suspect
My sins.

GUZMAN
           Nothing real, Sir, do dreams convey.
Dream, if you must, of your generous fiancée.

BERNARD
Even she fills my mind with worry and strife.

There are pitfalls and dangers in selecting a wife.
The fatal mistake—again—is what I fear.

GUZMAN
Picture Constance lying there, Bernard, lying here...

BERNARD
When for Constance my desire begins to revive,
I think: What if somehow my wife is still alive?
What if, one day, to punish me for my sin,
Julie returns? And before Constance and kin
And all the town, she reveals my crime?
Would revenge not be just, if revenge be her design?
She haunts me, Guzman, these three long years.
No sleep, but the blackness of guilt and fear.

GUZMAN
No talk of crime, Sir. This word should be banned.
Primo, remember this: You're an innocent man.
There is one fact, Sir, no judge could ignore:
Her betrayal of you. She was justly punished for
Her infidelity. Take heart. Be you brave.
Secundo: Do the dead return from the grave?
Use logic, Sir. Think of all the ways she might die.
There's starvation. There's thirst. In that sun, she would fry.
Or a storm might have got her. Or at the very least,
She was a savory meal for some wild, growling beast.

BERNARD
Will you stop!? The devil take your babbling tongue.

GUZMAN
Yes, Sir.

BERNARD
Three years I've kept secret what was done.
None suspected her fate, none knew of my shame.
She died a faithful wife, and I kept my good name.
As proof of my heart stands her monument. And yet.
'Tis monument to my own eternal regret.
And you, who dare talk of infidelity,
God help you if you've been unfaithful to me.

GUZMAN
Not a soul knows the truth. I swear on my life.
Only you and me. And...

BERNARD
And who?

GUZMAN
Your wife.

BERNARD
Her servant knows half, but that half she has kept
Secret, out of fear. I should take comfort, except...
What of whispers and rumors, lingering suspicion?
In the market, as I stroll, my ears strain to listen
For fragments of gossip, some pointed critique.
"Why has he not remarried?" I heard that last week.

GUZMAN
Soon you shall answer all questions on the topic.

BERNARD
You disapprove.

GUZMAN
Oh, marry away—if it's too late to stop it.
Although I feel moved, Sir, to offer some advice.
I'm an expert on women—but never on wives.
Avoid at all costs the matrimonial mistake
Of a legal quagmire from which you cannot extricate.

BERNARD
Constance is young, and fresh.

GUZMAN
Young. At least in years.
In love, she's a veteran. Decorated. Your fears
Should be raised. To put it plainly, in a word:
You're no chooser of women—and you're no match for *her*.
Now, if there were a dowry, your plans would make sense,
But in her case, the dowry would have to be immense.
No, into *your* money, Master, she'd like to get her claws.

BERNARD
I shall marry her, though money's not the cause.
Nor the physical charms of which she may boast.
My reason is simple: I want to banish a ghost.
   (Preparing to leave.)
I had hoped to meet Constance. I shall find her at home.

GUZMAN
Worse luck, if you do, Sir. She'll not be alone.

BERNARD
What's that?

GUZMAN
Surely it's just her youthful charm,
But she had that new stranger hanging on her arm.

BERNARD
Again?

GUZMAN
It could be, Sir, you've already lost her.

BERNARD
To that pretentious new fool? That overdressed impostor?
A charmer, a talker, a courtier-at-large.
They say he is part of the Duke's entourage.

GUZMAN
Frederic, they call him.

BERNARD
I call him worse.
A snake and a scoundrel. The man is a curse.
Their whispers and laughter, their long promenades.
Who knows what progress he already has made?

GUZMAN
A lot, probably.

BERNARD
A knave and a plotter. I see it in his eyes.
That's a man of no morals, of flattery and lies.
I shall call him on it. Guzman, this is war!

GUZMAN
I'd not advise a milit'ry campaign at his door.

Take the bull by the horns, and you may get gored.
They say that this Frederic is skilled with a sword.

BERNARD

Skilled?

GUZMAN
Quite skilled.

BERNARD
That's important information.

GUZMAN
Yes. I suggest we make a try at skillful negotiation.

BERNARD

I agree.

GUZMAN
You're no swordsman. With a blade, you're a hack.
But then, you're no lover, either. The art of sticking, you lack.

(GUZMAN chuckles at his own witticism, until he is silenced by a slap to the back of the head by BERNARD.)

BERNARD

My power lies elsewhere. Here in this town,
My good name is my currency, and my renown.
Thus, I have the mother. I've impressed her, you see,
With my stature and wealth. She'll give Constance to me.
Let this bellicose Frederic posture and swagger.
He might win in war, but not in nuptial matter!

(FREDERIC approaches, accompanied by his valet, OCTAVIUS. They are carrying an array of swords, with

which they are about to practice: the effect is that they appear armed to the teeth. GUZMAN sees them; BERNARD does not.)

GUZMAN

Sir.

BERNARD

The confidence flows.

GUZMAN

Sir?

BERNARD

I banish all fear.

GUZMAN

Sir!

BERNARD

What is it?

GUZMAN

It's him.

BERNARD

Who?

GUZMAN

He's here.

(BERNARD turns to see FREDERIC and OCTAVIUS, over-armed, staring confidently at him.)

SCENE FOUR

FREDERIC
Sir! I do charge you, by your "stature and wealth,"
To answer me this question: How goes your health?

BERNARD *(taken aback)*.
I am well, Sir, since you ask.

FREDERIC
     It comes as no surprise.
Vitality fair radiates from a young lover's eyes.
But of course, you'll need it.

BERNARD
     Need? What do you mean?

FREDERIC
He who would marry courts dangers yet unseen.

(As the conversation continues, GUZMAN and OCTA-VIUS draw aside. Wordlessly, they size each other up like two combatants, mirroring the attitude of their masters. They might get into a little stage business—card tricks for example, or disappearing coins, each trying to impress the other. FREDERIC, meanwhile, tries out his several swords.)

BERNARD
Life is full of risk.

FREDERIC
    And married life, doubly so.
It throws the humors out of whack, as all doctors know.

Strains the nerves and constitution, most tragically.
Oh, for marriage, you'll need health—in quantity.

BERNARD

A wife brings great happiness.

FREDERIC

And more, that is so.
But great happiness has a way of yielding greater woe.
To watch a loved one suffer leaves a scar that will endure.

BERNARD

Is it so? On that point, I shall have to take your word.
(Bowing.) Your humble servant.

(BERNARD begins to leave, but FREDERIC halts him.)

FREDERIC

Oh what pleasure would be mine!
To see you with wife. Someone cultured and refined,
Whose love might mirror the very passion in your soul,
Instruct you in tenderness and help to make you whole.
Her qualities would be the very legends of this place.
Oh! I picture such a woman even now in your embrace.

BERNARD

You'd do well to find a loving woman of your own.

FREDERIC

I've done so.

BERNARD

Have you, then?

FREDERIC
To you she's well known.

BERNARD
Explain yourself.

FREDERIC
You'll not like it.

BERNARD
Like what, pray tell?

FREDERIC
The truth—which, however, you should know full well.
I must tell you. As your friend, what could be fairer?
Sir: If you marry Constance—you shall have to share her.
 (A beat.)

BERNARD *(feigning amusement)*.
Your devotion to my Constance will constant be?
How admirable and amusing. You'll write her poetry.

FREDERIC
And more.

BERNARD
Send her gifts.

FREDERIC
Oh, more, much more.

BERNARD
Explain yourself. What is in this "more"?

FREDERIC
If you succeed—

BERNARD
"If"?

FREDERIC
—in winning Constance for your bride,
You'll have not one but two companions by your side.

BERNARD
You intend to call, then. How often?

FREDERIC
Oh, I should say,
Not more than two or three or four times a day.

BERNARD
Your proposal I find offensive.

FREDERIC
Proposal it is not.
Constance shall have what Constance shall want.

BERNARD
You anticipate a schedule? Certain appointed times—?

FREDERIC
No restrictions must apply to love so bold as mine.

BERNARD
What, at any hour of the night you might appear?
When she and I, in bed, we—?

FREDERIC
What?

BERNARD
We— Now see here!

FREDERIC
I shall see here—and there, both near and far.
What I have in view is the perfect *ménage à trois*.
I shall watch you from the shadows, listen as you pass,
Hear your sighs together, her every secret laugh.
Dream your dreams, say the words you leave unsaid.
Whensoe're it please me, I shall have her in my bed.

BERNARD
Stop there! Is it some fool you take me for?
You expect me to share the woman I adore?
You dare propose one sole wife between us—!

FREDERIC
Do you fear such arrangements might demean us?
'Tis common fashion, Sir, among the better kind.

BERNARD
Let fashion have its slaves, but never me or mine.
You annoy me, Sir. You begin to heat my bile.
What you propose and represent is all that I revile.
Take this as a warning, or take it as you please:
Enter by my door, and by my window you will leave.

FREDERIC
A man of strong emotion. Our Constance is well blessed.
Hers is very like the man I once possessed.

BERNARD

A man, say you?

FREDERIC

Did I?

BERNARD

Enough! My patience you abuse.
What your Duke may permit, Sir, I do refuse.
The royal court may emulate the ancient Greek nation,
But *this* town will never bow to sexual deviation!
Your humble servant.

(Exit BERNARD, with GUZMAN. OCTAVIUS and FREDERIC will shortly begin their fencing practice. Various thrusts and parries punctuate their conversation. OCTAVIUS is the teacher, FREDERIC the advanced student.)

FREDERIC

I have met the enemy, Octavius. The battle is engaged.

OCTAVIUS

Though it won't help your cause to send him off, enraged.

FREDERIC

More frustration Bernard exhibits than bravery.

OCTAVIUS

He worries about his Constance.

FREDERIC

Or her dowry.

OCTAVIUS
No, I think not. If you push him too hard,
You'll discover there is a fighting side to Bernard.
(Swordplay.)
Be cautious. I urge you.

FREDERIC
That, and cunning, I will be.
Full well I know this man and his tendencies.
He used violence in the past, and may so again.
I shall act the part of his affectionate friend.

OCTAVIUS
You're his rival for Constance. To him, you're a threat.
He'll defend his betrothed.

FREDERIC
She's not betrothed. Not yet.
(Swordplay.)

OCTAVIUS
Your improvement continues.

FREDERIC
My instruction goes apace.
I've an excellent teacher.

OCTAVIUS
Who knows his place?
(Swordplay.)

FREDERIC
From all she has told me, big tears she has cried,
Inconstant Constance will not soon be his bride.

Bernard she despises. His *attention* she desires.
She would gladly roast his heart on the roaring fires
Of her passion. It's a game, Octavius. Do you see?
And sweet Constance plays it most expertly.
There's Don Lope the Spaniard, Bernard and myself
As her three present suitors: trophies for her shelf.
  (Swordplay.)

OCTAVIUS
This game has its risks, both for you and for her.
I beg of you, Julie—

FREDERIC
Not "Julie"! "*Sir.*"
(A beat, as they glance around to make certain they have not been overheard.)
Caution, good Octavius, and presence of mind.
I will unmask myself, but all in good time.
To return to this place took me three long years.
I've overcome a great deal, but not all my fears.
When my husband abandoned me, his boat sailed away,
I fell to my knees. For my own death I prayed.

OCTAVIUS
But heaven refused you. Then a ship passed near,
Heard your cries and rescued you.

FREDERIC
My duty then was clear.
I made my way to Venice, assumed this disguise.

OCTAVIUS
And ceased to be a woman in your fellow men's eyes.

FREDERIC

As a man, I could move freely, my safety assured.
Again heaven helped me. I was granted a word
With the Duke of Modine, sovereign lord of these lands.
He befriended me. I placed my fate in his hands.
He was good to his Frederic, and at his behest
I joined him on his travels, not forgetting my quest.

OCTAVIUS

Now the Duke has returned here. Full circle you've come.

FREDERIC

The final stage of my journey now has begun:
I must uncover the truth, somehow must I learn,
Why my husband from lover to executioner did turn.

OCTAVIUS

But have you the courage to play this part?
You must rely on your reason, and not on your heart.
You forget you once loved him? Will your anger not show?

FREDERIC

To answer you honestly: I don't know.
I see him, and I am consumed with rage.
And with longing, too, for that golden age
When we loved, and loved dearly. All too brief.
Now my purpose is to capture and punish the thief
Who stole all I held worthy, my love and my life.

OCTAVIUS

Would you punish Bernard? Let him take a new wife.
In the eyes of the Church and the law, he is lost.

FREDERIC
The strategy is simple. But I am fearful of its cost.

OCTAVIUS
To yourself, is your meaning.

FREDERIC
Take it as you will.

OCTAVIUS
I take it to mean, some love is there still.

FREDERIC
Octavius—

(Swordplay. OCTAVIUS quickly overwhelms his student.)

OCTAVIUS
Poorly played. You let down your guard.

FREDERIC
My mind was distracted.

OCTAVIUS
With thoughts of Bernard.

FREDERIC
How changed he looks. There is a grimness to his eyes,
A cruelty new to his lips. I did scarcely recognize
His face. With such love it once did look upon mine.
He has aged not three, but ten years' time.
(A beat.)

OCTAVIUS
You charged me keep a secret—have I not obeyed?

FREDERIC
And I promise, you will one day be generously paid.

OCTAVIUS
In swordplay, you begged instruction. I've complied,
And taught you well.

FREDERIC
Which I do not deny.
My trust and gratitude, these you have earned.
Soon to the Duke's service you may return.

OCTAVIUS
Give me no payment, but this pledge, if you can:
To see me not as servant, but as a man.
Dearest Julie—

FREDERIC
No—

OCTAVIUS
I must speak.

FREDERIC
Hold your tongue!

OCTAVIUS
I will not! Men too have hearts. May I have none?
For one reason alone am I here by your side.
This reason, Madam, I no longer wish to hide.

FREDERIC
I seek out Bernard—

OCTAVIUS
The man who sought your death.

FREDERIC
He was taken perhaps by madness—

OCTAVIUS
Is *your* madness less?
This battle within you, that overtakes your soul,
That blinds you to me, that makes you play this role—
Is there yet a woman beneath this disguise?

FREDERIC
I did believe it.

OCTAVIUS
Julie. Give up this enterprise
Before it damns you. Come away now with me.

FREDERIC
Once was I damned. If again I must be,
My fate I accept. You must do so, as well,
Octavius. Although I can not tell
Where my quest will end, or where, my life,
While I live, I am yet this man's wife.

OCTAVIUS
I'm sorry, for us both.

FREDERIC
More wit, and less apology,

Dear friend. The task is to advance this rivalry,
And learn the secret reasons behind his crime,
Before Bernard a husband is, for the second time.

OCTAVIUS
By what method? What now will you do?

FREDERIC
At present, loyal Octavius...I haven't got a clue.

END OF ACT ONE

ACT TWO

SCENE ONE

(Enter CONSTANCE, breathlessly, followed by BEATRICE.)

CONSTANCE
Frederic! At last. Do you know what I place at risk,
Running madly to meet you in public like this?
Have I abandoned all reason? Have I lost my mind?
Have you no pity? I am running out of time!
Frederic. My wedding approaches. Will you let this heart
Forever be enslaved to such a man as Bernard?

FREDERIC
I would sooner pluck it out with this, my own hand—

CONSTANCE
Your passion, what comfort—but I'd rather see a *plan*.
Mother has betrothed me. The time for words is past.

FREDERIC
Sweet Constance. Do you doubt that I am equal to the task?

(CONSTANCE, on the verge of an embrace, restrains herself.)

CONSTANCE
Halt! Before I reveal the high matter of my heart,
Give me privacy. Let the low ones depart.

(BEATRICE and OCTAVIUS depart, but not without a disdainful glance or two at CONSTANCE.)

FREDERIC
With heaven as my witness, I do swear it by my life:
I shall never let Bernard take Constance for his wife.
The thought, in fact, does sicken me. Therefore, this vow:
I shall prevent it!

CONSTANCE
I rejoice to hear it. But *how*?

FREDERIC
How, you say? Madam. In the...masculine fashion.

CONSTANCE
The sword!

FREDERIC
The sword?

CONSTANCE
How I love a man of action!

FREDERIC
The sword?

CONSTANCE
Oh, how dramatic. Over me—a duel!
But I forbid you—

FREDERIC
Thank God.

CONSTANCE
To be excessively cruel.
No butchering. A few holes. Perhaps one vicious slice.
And no corpses, I pray you. Simple crippling will suffice.

FREDERIC
Constance. I must tell you, despite all you see and hear,
That, I may not be, in truth, precisely what I appear.
I have a certain exterior, but truly, little more.
You see in me a man of courage. But are you sure?
I don't wish to mislead you, to say anything untrue—

CONSTANCE
O! Frederic. Heaven no longer makes such men as you!

FREDERIC
That's just my point—

CONSTANCE
Withdraw your weapon. Now.

FREDERIC
My what?

CONSTANCE
I must see it! And admire it!

FREDERIC
Here?

CONSTANCE
Now!

FREDERIC
Madam, control yourself, I beg you.

CONSTANCE
No! I shall not!

(To FREDERIC's horror, CONSTANCE turns away, covers her eyes and gropes, though prudently, of course, in the general direction of his waist—where she finds the hilt of his sword. She withdraws it.)

CONSTANCE
Instrument of power, what terror thou hast wrought!

FREDERIC
That's sharp, be careful—

CONSTANCE
To Bernard, I prefer my death!

FREDERIC
Madam, please—

CONSTANCE
Must I pierce this innocent breast!?

FREDERIC
No!

CONSTANCE
Swear then upon it.

FREDERIC
Your breast?

CONSTANCE

> The sword!
> Your pledge of undying love—this shall be my reward.

FREDERIC

Constance. No man could deny how your charms attract.
But to fully please you, there is something that I lack.
That is— What I mean to say—

CONSTANCE

> Dear one, do not dismay.
> Though my beauty seem impregnable, you shall find a way!
> Of course, I guard my honor. But in love, what might occur...

FREDERIC

Your honor is safe with me. Of that you may be sure.

CONSTANCE

My champion. You may kiss me.

FREDERIC

> Here?

CONSTANCE

> We are alone.

FREDERIC

Someone may come—

CONSTANCE
Close your eyes, and it is done.

(CONSTANCE yanks FREDERIC into a kiss. A beat. FREDERIC breaks away.)

FREDERIC
What was that?

CONSTANCE
Cupid's arrow. Now there's no stopping.

FREDERIC
I heard a sound.

CONSTANCE
Your breeches button, popping.

(Again, she pulls him into a kiss. A beat. CONSTANCE might try a not-too-discreet hand to FREDERIC's crotch. FREDERIC, alarmed, breaks away. CONSTANCE, puzzled, glances at her hand.)

FREDERIC
Madam, please—

CONSTANCE
My love, do you resist?

FREDERIC
It's just—indigestion.

CONSTANCE
I can help.

FREDERIC
No.

CONSTANCE

I insist. Declare your noble passion— Now!

(Again, a kiss from CONSTANCE; FREDERIC struggles against it, unsuccessfully. Unseen by either, OCTAVIUS has entered. He approaches, waits a beat, then clears his throat. Startled, the two embracers disengage.)

OCTAVIUS
Sir, I must intrude.

FREDERIC
We were just talking.

OCTAVIUS
So I conclude.

Of philosophy?

CONSTANCE
And since when do servants moralize?

OCTAVIUS
My Lady, since noble hearts go forth in disguise. My Lord, the Duke.

FREDERIC
Where?

OCTAVIUS
You must not be late.

FREDERIC
Late?

OCTAVIUS
For your meeting.

FREDERIC
Yes! I dare not hesitate.
(Hurries away, then hurriedly returns.)
Madam, have no fear. From Bernard I shall defend you.
To see you fully satisfied—know that I intend to.
(With a grimace at his own phrase, then a bow.)
Your devoted servant.

(Exit FREDERIC and OCTAVIUS.)

SCENE TWO

CONSTANCE *(calling after him).*
My fate is in your hands!

(A beat; BEATRICE appears.)

CONSTANCE
On earth, is there any stranger nature than a man's?
He is shy, somewhat nervous. Lacking in perfection.
And too discreet by half, to withhold his true affection.
Yet I see his potential. Valorous, brave and true.
Though I admit this is a man with a problem or two.
'Tis odd, but in his nature, I sense something of my own.

BEATRICE
That should tell you, my lady, you're better off alone.

CONSTANCE
Not so. I know a real man, and a lover, when I see one.

BEATRICE
Unless your luck's against you, that fop will never be one.
Oh, that's a flatterer, I tell you, a phony and a cheat.
He's hiding something, that one. His eyes are all deceit.

CONSTANCE
I find him clever and quite witty. Learned and refined.

BEATRICE
Pray that to your bed he brings more than just his mind.
He is unworthy of you, Madam, yet you treat him as some God.
I see him with unblinded eye. Believe me, he is flawed.
Eyes too deep, lips too large. His nose, much too thin.
And beware the evil omen: not a hair upon his chin!

CONSTANCE
Superstitious woman! Your judgment's much too hard.
Frederic isn't perfect—but would you have me take Bernard?

BEATRICE
Madam, no, upon my life—and perhaps, upon yours, too.
Take my advice, I pray you: Don Lope's the man for you.

(Enter, from behind, DON LOPE.)

CONSTANCE
Oh, Beatrice.

BEATRICE
Hear me, Madam. His love for you is strong.
A man of noble passion. How could that be wrong?
He is brusque at times, but honest. A soldier's life he's had.

CONSTANCE
I want a husband, not a general. Don Lope. Are you mad?

(BEATRICE sees DON LOPE, tries to signal CONSTANCE.)

CONSTANCE
Of all the men in France, he's the first that I would flee.
If he's learned of my engagement, he'll be furious with me.

DON LOPE
Señorita.

(CONSTANCE, startled, nearly jumps into BEATRICE's arms.)

DON LOPE
I come to hear you deny the news.
That Bernard wins your hand, and your heart I do lose.
I know this is some rumor. A lie. It could not be.
"No, no," I say, "My Constance, she is promised to *me*.
She would not betray me, drive a sword through my heart."

CONSTANCE *(having recovered her composure).*
Don Lope. Dearest. People make such remarks.
It is folly to believe everything one has heard.

DON LOPE
Then it's a lie?

CONSTANCE
Did I say that?

BEATRICE
She did not use that word.

DON LOPE
Then it's true?

CONSTANCE
Well...

BEATRICE
To be honest...

CONSTANCE
Less untrue than not.

(A beat.)

DON LOPE
One question.

CONSTANCE
Yes?

DON LOPE
Have you been won... Or been *bought!?*

CONSTANCE
Oh!

DON LOPE
Bernard's money is what has turned your head!

CONSTANCE
How could you think that?

DON LOPE
How could *you* strike me dead?
You murder my affection. You wound my very soul!

CONSTANCE
But mother has betrothed me. I must do as I am told.
I go to this wedding as I would go to my own death,
With thoughts of Don Lope here, deep in my breast.
Dearest, believe me. I would never cause you pain.
I treasure the heat and power of your flame.
I have seen the passion glowing deep in your eyes.
I have gloried in the sound of your manly sighs.
My captain! Your willing prisoner I would be.
But there's Bernard. And my mother. And...reality.

DON LOPE
To lose you, Constance—I would lose my own life!

CONSTANCE
If I marry—quite unwilling—you *would* lose a wife.
But think, my brave soldier, what you would gain:
A mistress, and a rich one...

DON LOPE *(rejecting her)*.
Are you quite insane?
You dare to imagine I would share you with another?
That I would accept defeat and become your lover?

CONSTANCE
These transports of emotion, I find them distasteful.
You rage to no avail. It's really quite wasteful.
Calm reason, Don Lope, this would serve you well.

DON LOPE

Reason? You reason your way straight to hell!
I shall have justice. I swear by this sign:
  (He makes the cross.)
As I am Don Lope— Wench, you will be mine!

(Exit CONSTANCE, insulted and angry.)

DON LOPE

By all the saints in heaven! That woman, she is hard.
I don't believe my own ears. Marry Bernard?

BEATRICE

It shall never be.

DON LOPE
What? What is that you say?

BEATRICE

I am forbidden to talk.

DON LOPE
  Beatrice. I know the way
To loosen your tongue. A ducat. Now tell me.

BEATRICE

One lonely ducat, Señor, could hardly compel me
To betray my lady.

DON LOPE
  Then I make it two.
Tell me what you know, Beatrice. Do.

BEATRICE
Two little coins? A childless couple. How sad.

DON LOPE
Here is progeny. Take it, before I get mad.

BEATRICE
A family of three. God forgive them their sins,
And bless their fine house, by sending them...twins.

DON LOPE
Five ducats!?

BEATRICE
A bargain, Señor, to learn your true fate.

DON LOPE
This is robbery!

BEATRICE
As you wish, Sir.
(She makes to hand him back the coins.)

DON LOPE
No. Wait.
Five ducats it is. Now tell me all you know.

BEATRICE
To such generous persuasion, I could not say no.
The truth is this: Though Bernard seeks her hand,
Constance will not have him, for she loves another man.

DON LOPE
Who?

BEATRICE
Dare I say?

DON LOPE
Speak now, or lose that tongue!
(DON LOPE withdraws his sword.)

BEATRICE *(frightened).*
Yes, yes, Sir, I speak! Frederic is the one.

DON LOPE
Frederic! And does he love Constance in return?

BEATRICE
So he declares. And from what I can learn,
He vows to stop the marriage, and make her his own.

DON LOPE
Not while there is life yet in this flesh and bone.
Fine phrases and fashion have turned her head.
But how fine will this Frederic look to her, dead?

BEATRICE
Don Lope, I pray you, be cautious and wise.

DON LOPE
You, Madam pirate, shall be my ears and eyes.

BEATRICE
I dare not, Don Lope.

DON LOPE
You shall be well paid.

BEATRICE
In that case, Señor, I am your most loyal maid.
(Exit BEATRICE.)

DON LOPE
I go to find Frederic, whose love she so prizes.
Man to man, I shall show to him what my device is
For convincing a lover, a mistake he has made.
My argument lies here, on the edge of my blade.
(Exit DON LOPE.)

SCENE THREE

(Later that day. GUZMAN, hanging out at the fountain, wasting time. Enter BERNARD.)

BERNARD
Guzman! The news! Is it not wondrously fine?
Glorious! Miraculous! Do you not find it sublime?

GUZMAN
To be full honest, Master, I don't find it at all.
I'll search, if you insist. Is it large, or is it small?

BERNARD
He is gone, the old hangman. Called to Paris by the king.

GUZMAN
Which hangman is that, Sir?

BERNARD
Oh, what a marvelous thing!
All my problems are solved, Guzman. Do you not rejoice?

GUZMAN
Well, Sir, I, uh— Do I have a choice?

BERNARD
Heaven assures my safety. Perhaps the hand of Fate
Has intervened in my behalf, to raise up my estate.
Mizanti, the old judge—he stepped down from his post.
There now. Is it clear?

GUZMAN
Well—

BERNARD
         Is it?

GUZMAN
              Almost.

BERNARD
This judgeship is my salvation, Guzman. And what is more,
I shall request it this day.

GUZMAN
         Good idea, Sir. Who for?

BERNARD
Who? Why, you hollow-headed sot. For me.

GUZMAN
You? A judge?

BERNARD
        The perfect move. Don't you see?
If despite my precautions, the truth should come out,

If someone should come forth with accusation and doubt
Of my late wife's demise and matters in this regard,
He must make the charge to me, Royal Magistrate, Bernard.

GUZMAN
Oh, ho! That is *good!*

BERNARD
Is it not?

GUZMAN
Oh, it is, for a fact.
But there's one small problem, Sir.

BERNARD
And what is that?

GUZMAN
As your servant, my duty is to point out this flaw:
You haven't the foggiest notion of the law.

BERNARD
Objection sustained. Your point is not moot.
Though for knowledge, I possess the proper substitute.
Money, Guzman. This office shall be bought.

GUZMAN
I hesitate to express this, Sir, but...I think not.
'Tis the Duke of Modine who alone has the right
To appoint to this judgeship whosoever he might.
And the Duke, being rich, and right honest, as well,
Appoints his judges on merit. He won't offer to sell.

BERNARD
Philosophers say merit's but an unlettered fool,
Unless money walks with him and leads him to school.
The Duke may be honest, but the Duke is a man.
Money will speak to him, as only money can.
The robes of a judge, once properly bought,
Will suit me well. Do you agree?

GUZMAN
                         Dare I not?

BERNARD
I'll make a competent judge. I have ample common sense.
I can easily devise punishments to match any offense.
See the guilty tremble before me, and lose all hope.
In sympathy, I give a choice: death in prison, or the rope.
A reputation for fairness. My name shall be known.
Something judicial will reside in me, solid as stone.

GUZMAN
That'd be your heart, Sir.

BERNARD
                  This judgeship will be mine,
If I overpay its value by ten or twenty times.
And I know the man who will help me procure it.
I shall make a friend of Frederic—if I can endure it.
He's a favorite of the Duke—a favorite what, they do not say.

GUZMAN
You can find out for yourself. I see him coming this way.

SCENE FOUR

(Enter FREDERIC.)

BERNARD

Good Sir.

FREDERIC

Your servant, Sir.

BERNARD

If you please. A word.

FREDERIC

To speak with you, Sir, is my pleasure, be assured.
I fear I gave offense with my too-bold proposal.
I meant to cast no shadow on your glorious betrothal.
I pray you, give me means, Sir, to amend
This grievous error. For I so wish to be your friend.

BERNARD

Friendship, Sir, between us might one day come to be.
For there is one little favor you could do for me.

FREDERIC

Ask, and it is yours.

BERNARD
The Duke. You have his ear?

FREDERIC

I am so blessed.

BERNARD
So you are. Now listen here.
The office of royal magistrate has now a vacancy.
I wish the Duke to fill it.

FREDERIC
With whom, Sir?

BERNARD
Sir, with me.

(A beat. FREDERIC nearly chokes.)

BERNARD
Are you ill, Sir?

FREDERIC
No, no.

BERNARD
You suffer from catarrh?

FREDERIC
No, I was overcome to think how fortunate we are
That henceforth in your person our justice might reside.
The very concept fills me with...

GUZMAN
Phlegm?

BERNARD
Pride.

FREDERIC
That's the word.

BERNARD
Then I may count upon your aid?

FREDERIC
Dear Bernard, of course.

BERNARD
I insist that you be paid.
No, no, I've weighed the evidence, and I have decreed.
Two hundred ducats I award, for your personal need.

FREDERIC
The promise of your friendship is all that I require.
Yet: To hold this sacred office: How deep is your desire?

BERNARD
How deep?

GUZMAN
Bottomless.

BERNARD
Profound.

FREDERIC
Ah, I do so admire
A man of conviction.

GUZMAN
That's him.

FREDERIC

                        Still, the Duke will ask
Whether you, friend Bernard, are equal to the task.
My meaning, Sir: Are you quite certain you possess
The courage to send man—or woman—to her death?

(BERNARD, for a moment, looks as if he will be sick. He sits by the fountain.)

FREDERIC

Are you ill, Sir? You look pale. Perhaps my questions bore you.
Ah, I have just the thing. A splash of water to restore you.

(FREDERIC, from behind him, pushes BERNARD's face into the water, holds his head down. Some thrashing from BERNARD.)

FREDERIC

Be not dismayed, Sir, at your mind's slight hesitation.
Your doubt is soon flushed out, with a little irrigation.
   (Lifts BERNARD's head.)
Better now? Again. Why not?
   (Back in.)
                        This works miraculously.
All the better doctors swear by hydro-therapy.

(Again he lifts BERNARD's head. Sputtering and angry, BERNARD jumps to his feet.)

FREDERIC

No! Do not thank me, Sir, for this restorative anointment.
I must fly, to beg the Duke for your judicial appointment.
   (Exit FREDERIC.)

GUZMAN
He said "woman."

BERNARD
And "death."

GUZMAN
You don't think he knew?

BERNARD
I'll get even with that bastard if it's the last thing I do.

(Exit BERNARD, wetly, followed by GUZMAN.)

SCENE FIVE

(Re-enter FREDERIC, stealthily, watching after the departing BERNARD and GUZMAN.)

FREDERIC
The taste of revenge will be sweet. That was but a drop.
Yet, I worry at my thirst. Once begun, where will it stop?
I was happy here, with him. But is it Bernard I miss?
Or two people once in love who no longer exist?
My heart, I won't deny, knows some feeling for him still.
Julie, be firm. Let not your heart overrule your will.
I wish that it were madness, some malady or spell
That drove him to his act. I could believe it well.
Oh, what do I want? Punishment? Payment for his crime?
Or to reclaim a love that once was rightfully mine?
All is stolen from me—my life, my husband, my home.
I am outcast. No place or pity for a woman, alone.
He plans now to remarry. I feel the fury in me rise.

Act II LOVERS AND EXECUTIONERS

He will not remarry. I have my own plans to devise.
So the man would be a judge?... Wait. Now comes the light!
Yes! Yes, yes, yes! This bitch still has some bite!
Bernard's vain ambition—there's the tool I need
To uncover what lies beneath his murderous deed.

(CONSTANCE appears.)

FREDERIC
Ah, Constance approaches. Revenge, did I say?
Bernard's true punishment is bouncing right this way.
(FREDERIC exits, hastily.)

END OF ACT TWO

ACT THREE

SCENE ONE

(CONSTANCE appears, followed closely by BEATRICE. They halt. CONSTANCE sends BEATRICE forward to reconnoiter. BEATRICE, advances cautiously, looks around, then signals for CONSTANCE to join her.)

BEATRICE
The storm has passed. Don Lope's gone.

(Enter CONSTANCE, cautiously.)

CONSTANCE
                            Are you sure?
Heaven save me from that raging toreador.
The one I disdain refuses all restraint,
While the one I adore acts the holy saint.
And the worst of the three, my supposed spouse,
Wants me as furniture for his empty house.
Bernard begs to meet—so reads his letter sent.
I shall have to listen now to his matrimonial lament.

BEATRICE *(dramatically)*.
Woman or man, cursèd be in equal part,
When the plague of love doth grip the heart!

CONSTANCE
What was that?

BEATRICE
Nothing.

CONSTANCE
"Nothing," you say?
Now I have a poet where once I had a maid?

BEATRICE
I offer, as comfort, a comforting word—

CONSTANCE
What do *you* know about love? Don't be absurd.

BEATRICE
I know more than the next, and well I might,
For I listen to you whine, day and night.
You sigh and moan, collapse upon your bed,
Call for heaven's mercy, and wish you were dead,
Nourish yourself on the tears that you weep,
While I am forbidden a decent night's sleep.

CONSTANCE
So then. *This* is the sympathy I receive,
While from sentence of death I await a reprieve?
To be married forever to a man I despise:
Do you wonder the thought brings tears to these eyes?
A woman has no power, save once in her life,
When men come begging to make her a wife.
I'll use this brief power, and choose my fate,
Defend my own future, before it's too late.
With the weapon of my youth, bravely and bold—

BEATRICE
Here comes your chance, Madam. Play well your role!

(Enter GUZMAN, carrying a wig.)

GUZMAN *(ceremoniously).*
M'Lady! As the sun does o'erwhelm the starry skies,
So too bright Bernard, in courtly guise.
Prepare now your heart, and shield your eyes!

(Enter BERNARD, dressed in some attempt at "fashion" —an over-embroidered coat, painfully new shoes. Worse, he wears a sword, which proves cumbersome, threatens to trip him up, etc. CONSTANCE, although suitably amazed at the sight, chooses to ignore her suitor's arrival.)

BERNARD
This is doomed to failure.

GUZMAN
                Sir, play well your part:
A bold, attacking style will win her heart.

BERNARD *(adjusting his sword).*
Must I wear this damned thing?

GUZMAN
                        Sir, the effect
Is palpable. A deadly weapon'll earn her respect.
A little intimidation, she's in your bed the faster.
The young wench of today longs to be mastered.

BERNARD
I must be mad. By my servant, convinced
To dress like some perfumed Turkish prince...

GUZMAN
Sir, the very latest fashion. You look... extraordinaire.
Now, if you'd only agree to put on the hair—

BERNARD
I'll not wear that monstrosity!

GUZMAN
Sir—

BERNARD
No!
There are certain lengths to which I will not go.

GUZMAN
As you wish.

BERNARD
Now what?

GUZMAN
Stoke her flame. Feed her fire.

BERNARD
She's not a cooking stove—

GUZMAN
I discreetly retire.
Oh, and don't forget their need of poetry.
Sprinkle your speech with amorous imagery.

BERNARD
Are you *certain*—?

GUZMAN
    Is not love my special bailiwick?
I am one man who knows how to use his... Quick,
Stand tall there. Look confident and firm.
Her exterior is ice. Yet her heart does burn.

(GUZMAN withdraws a respectful distance; BEATRICE does the same. They observe the mating ritual, and occasionally give signals of encouragement, etc.)

BERNARD
Constance. Good day.

CONSTANCE
    Is it? Very well. If you say.

BERNARD
So I do. Though you may not see it that way,
Feeling timid and nervous, a slight touch of dread,
As you prepare to enter the sanctum of my bed.

CONSTANCE
"Sanctum"?

(GUZMAN signals his encouragement to BERNARD.)

BERNARD
    Unschooled in love, 'tis natural to know fear.
But I shall instruct you. Your duties will be clear.

CONSTANCE
How fortunate am I that with such grace
Bernard so expertly shows Constance her place.

(A beat, as BERNARD struggles with his weapon.)

                    CONSTANCE
Are you having some trouble?

                    BERNARD
                        What?

                    CONSTANCE
                            Your sword.

                    BERNARD
Oh, this? My milit'ry skills I have lately ignored.
But I renew my acquaintance with the warring art.

                    CONSTANCE
How fearsome for your rivals.

                    BERNARD
                        Yes. Ow!

                    CONSTANCE
                            Careful. It's sharp.

(More signals from GUZMAN.)

                    BERNARD
We were speaking of love.

                    CONSTANCE
                        No. "Duties."

                    BERNARD
                            As I said.

CONSTANCE
And mine, no doubt, shall be fulfilled in your bed?

BERNARD
As naked you lie beneath me, remember this the while:
I awake in you the woman, and banish the child.

CONSTANCE
You make it sound so...

BERNARD
Romantic?

CONSTANCE
                Educational.

BERNARD
                Well said.
I've ever liked a woman who can use her head.
Of learned women, I fully approve. In fact—

(Signal of warning from GUZMAN.)

CONSTANCE
Bernard.

BERNARD
Yes, Constance?

CONSTANCE
        Tell me: What is that?

BERNARD
What?

CONSTANCE
What you're wearing.

BERNARD
This?

CONSTANCE
Heaven knows,
An aging widower might exaggerate his clothes,
But really, Bernard. You do look the fool.

BERNARD
It's the very latest fashion.

CONSTANCE
Where? In Istanbul?
As a young woman who goes occasionally outside,
I do think of style. And I do have my pride.

(More warnings from GUZMAN, here and throughout.)

BERNARD
Or vanity, you mean. Where's pride in the act
Of taking a year's income and wearing it on your back?

CONSTANCE
To what better purpose, Sir, might income be put,
Than to adorn a woman gloriously, from head to foot?

BERNARD
It's laughable, the effort that is wasted these days
In hopes of being noticed in the courtly parade.
Peacocks and simpletons, with no thought in their brains
But what color my parasol if, tragically, it rains.

CONSTANCE
Whereas, with *your* suit, a downpour might improve it.

BERNARD
This? What do you suggest?

CONSTANCE
As a first step, remove it.

BERNARD *(taking off his coat)*.
I should never have put it on. One gets bad advice,
And so we're made a fool.

CONSTANCE
Not once, but twice.
Have you no wigs?

BERNARD
I reject the former.

CONSTANCE
For a balding man like you, would not a wig be warmer?

BERNARD
Wigs stifle the brain. I find them a curse.

CONSTANCE
Your brain, unstifled: I can scarce imagine worse.
Unsuited and unsuitable, Sir. You lack taste.

BERNARD
My first wife disdained such self-indulgent waste.
She found no need, perfect strangers to impress
With empty wit and a fashionable new dress.

No powders and pomades, oils, eaus and creams,
No witchcraft of turning "what is" to "what seems."
She read the philosophers. Her Latin she knew.
Her pleasures were many, her complaints were few.
Yet her beauty was renowned. She'd have taught you pride.

CONSTANCE
What a pity for both of us that your dear wife died.

BERNARD
Yes. A pity. Too true—for me, at least.

CONSTANCE
How touching.

(GUZMAN signals, gives BERNARD the next topic.)

BERNARD
What? Oh, yes. The wedding feast.
Now, when we're wed—

CONSTANCE
"If."

BERNARD
"If." We'll have guests.
Though not many.

CONSTANCE
Four hundred.

BERNARD
What!?

CONSTANCE

More or less.
I've made a list.

BERNARD

Four hundred? That's—exaggeration.
To begin our marriage on a such note of ostentation—

CONSTANCE

If it begins at all. I have yet to agree.

BERNARD

Your mother is in favor.

CONSTANCE

Is it mother or me
You are courting? Four hundred. I am firm.

BERNARD

No. To their own homes, let them return.

CONSTANCE

Absurd! And we—no food, no wine?

BERNARD

This, instead:
We shall feast upon each other, as we jump into my bed.

CONSTANCE

To but think of such a menu, I am stricken with gas.

BERNARD

You resist all my proposals.

CONSTANCE
Sir, to the last.

BERNARD *(a beat, appealing to her reason).*
The sacrament of marriage— Constance, please understand.
We must swear our worthiness before God and man.
I have been wed once. It weighs on my mind,
To ask heaven's blessing a second time.
And a large wedding, the crowds— I must confess,
In public celebration, I am not at my best.

CONSTANCE
The groom is more nervous than the virgin bride.

BERNARD
With a small, private service—would you not be satisfied?

(The question elicits laughter from BEATRICE and GUZMAN. A glance from CONSTANCE silences them.)

CONSTANCE
No.

BERNARD
Let us plan our future with present sacrifice,
Be prudent in our actions, exemplary in our lives.
We can know happiness. Even joy can be ours.
And Constance, did you know, in a matter of hours,
I shall be named judge? You shall be the spouse
Of a magistrate. Prestige and honor upon our house.
The mistakes of the past will all be overcome—

CONSTANCE
I'd love to hear your lecture, but I'm afraid I must run.

(Exit CONSTANCE, followed by BEATRICE. BERNARD disarms, GUZMAN helps.)

BERNARD
Guzman. Take this cursed sword. Let it be retired.
The interview, I fear, left something to be desired.

GUZMAN
Yes. Constance.

BERNARD
  At courting women, I've no talent, none.
I'm a pitiable figure. And for pity, she's too young.
What do I know of love? That it shatters like glass.
Betrayal and revenge—these are the facts.
Pity and forgiveness are a young lover's dream.
God, how I've changed in three years. I hardly seem
Myself anymore. My eyes, gone cold and hard.
My reflection's a stranger, plays the part of Bernard.

(FREDERIC has entered, from behind, during the last lines. OCTAVIUS follows.)

SCENE TWO

FREDERIC
Oh, what vision is this? Some spirit of the air?
Bernard? Don't tell me. You've changed your hair.

BERNARD
Frederic. I see you have returned at last.
Tell me. What news?

FREDERIC
I saw the Duke on your behalf.

BERNARD
Oh, loyal friend. I shall never forget you, I swear.

FREDERIC
The Duke was quite gracious. He listened with care
As I spoke of your qualities. Your honesty and trust,
Your will to be firm, even harsh, if you must.
I used praises as glowing as could be expected.

BERNARD
And what did he say?

FREDERIC
"Stay to lunch." I accepted.
We spoke of weighty matters. I chose the lamb.
The conversation intensified. The Duke had the ham.
He demanded my opinions, whether I agreed or no.
I answered frankly—over an exquisite Bordeaux.

BERNARD
But what did he say about *me?*

FREDERIC
About you?
"Bernard," mused the Duke. "Yes. His family I knew.
A fine, upstanding man. A credit to the town."

BERNARD
And then?

FREDERIC
And then? And then we sat down
In the library. The Duke, with infinite tact,
Cleared his throat and decided... upon a fine Armagnac.
Delicious.

BERNARD
But what did he say about my request?

FREDERIC
We have a new judge.

BERNARD
Dear friend! At last, success!

FREDERIC
One problem.

BERNARD
Money. I must pay a certain sum?
A few hundred ducats and the deal is done.
Gladly! For I am judge! Oh, what a glorious day!
Frederic, I shall remember you.

FREDERIC
Yes. I dare say.
Poor Bernard.

BERNARD
How's that? "Poor"?

FREDERIC
Accept my apology.

BERNARD

Your what?

FREDERIC
As town magistrate, the Duke appointed...me.

BERNARD

You?

FREDERIC
Of course, I refused. But he wouldn't hear it.

BERNARD

You!?

FREDERIC
He admires me too much, I do fear it.

BERNARD
You deceitful snake! You arrogant slave!
The judgeship for yourself? You traitorous knave!
I swear by my honor, you'll pay for this act.
Henceforth, you traitor—watch your back!

(Exit BERNARD and GUZMAN.)

SCENE THREE

FREDERIC

Is he not rare?

OCTAVIUS
Again, he threatens violence.

FREDERIC
But I have the means to reduce him to silence.
Before the law, let us see what arrogance remains.
Octavius. Arrest Bernard. Bring him to me in chains.

OCTAVIUS
But, Madam—

FREDERIC
No!

OCTAVIUS
The consequence of this act—?

FREDERIC
The battle is his who boldly presses the attack.
As he did mine, now I decide his fate.
I shall be firm, as I'm a woman—and a magistrate.

(Exit OCTAVIUS.)

FREDERIC
At last, with heaven's help, the thing goes well.
(Enter DON LOPE.)

DON LOPE
Frederic. Stand firm.

FREDERIC
Oh, dammit to hell...

DON LOPE
The rumor I have heard: Dare you deny it?

FREDERIC
Which rumor is that?

DON LOPE
No, no. Do not try it.
Sir! Do you hope to make Constance your wife?

FREDERIC
To keep her from Bernard, I would risk my life.

DON LOPE
That, scoundrel Frenchman, is a risk you do run!
(Drawing his sword.)
Now shall I finish what you have begun!

FREDERIC
Are you mad?

DON LOPE
Furious!

FREDERIC
That's not what I meant!

DON LOPE
Too late for meaning. Dissembler, repent!

(Swordplay. FREDERIC mounts a decent defense, and manages to avoid her attacker.)

FREDERIC
You're making a mistake, I swear by the gods!

DON LOPE
En garde! You deceitful eater of frogs!

FREDERIC
I'm a dangerous swordsman. I should alert you.
Be careful, Don Lope. I don't wish to hurt you.

(With a cry, DON LOPE makes another run at her; she ducks, retreats around the fountain, etc.)

DON LOPE
Defend yourself, villain! Fight like a man!

FREDERIC
Impossible!

DON LOPE
Vile coward!

FREDERIC
You wouldn't understand.

(DON LOPE makes another run; same business.)

DON LOPE
"Dangerous swordsman," eh?

FREDERIC
You risk your death—

DON LOPE
The only danger I run is to run out of breath!

(Same business.)

FREDERIC
Halt! If you kill me, you kill a royal magistrate!

DON LOPE *(with a bow).*
Oh. And *I* am Lope ben Ali, Arabian potentate.
(A cry, and he returns to the attack.)

FREDERIC
I am your friend, Don Lope. Your rival is Bernard—!

DON LOPE
You expect me to fall for that ploy? En garde!

(Same business. Finally, FREDERIC loses her sword, and DON LOPE has her pinned.)

DON LOPE *(sneeringly).*
No hope for a nation of men raised on cheese...!

FREDERIC
My interest in Constance is not what it seems—

DON LOPE
You don't sound so confident, my bold courtier.

FREDERIC
Your beloved will never be mine, I do swear!
Constance and I are two halves, truth be told,
Joined together would make an imperfect whole.
There is more to my person than meets the eye—

DON LOPE
Or less, I would say. But if this be some lie...

FREDERIC
On my honor I pledge, before this night is through,
Constance will have no suitor, save you.
Bernard and I both, we withdraw from the field.
And though my reasons must remain concealed,
I act in your interests. She can be your wife.
Or on the point of your sword, I yield my life.

DON LOPE
To carve you like venison. I have a mind to do it.
Instead, I show mercy. But—I hold you to it,
The bargain we have made.

FREDERIC
                You will have satisfaction.

DON LOPE
Or your funeral will be this town's next attraction.
(Exit DON LOPE.)

FREDERIC
Don't gallop so, my heart. We've escaped his blade.
I must be mad to continue this masquerade.
A captain full of threats; a husband full of menace.
These barbarous men. I should have stayed in Venice.
Fear does advise me, bring an end to this game.
But then my honor reminds me why I came.
'Tis not at all a game. My future is at stake.

(As she finishes her last lines, BERNARD appears, a prisoner, in chains and blindfolded.)

FREDERIC

Then I too am barbarous, if that's what it shall take.
My husband thinks me dead, his crime well hid.
But here stands the judge, to uncover what he did.
Leave me, scruples, compassion, all good sense.
Let me revel now in my just revenge!
Prepare yourself, husband. Your trial now begins.
And your victim demands payment for your sins.
Let us see how well guilt maintains his disguise,
When for once, in the wife, justice does reside.

END OF ACT THREE

ACT FOUR

SCENE ONE

(A judge's chambers. OCTAVIUS helps JULIE/FREDERIC don her robes and other judicial accessories. In the background stands BERNARD, bound and blindfolded.)

OCTAVIUS
I wondered once, Ma— "Sir"—if you were equal to this task.

FREDERIC
Call me "Your Honor."

OCTAVIUS
But now I must ask
Whether you go too far. He is guilty, that is true.
Must the next act of cruelty come from you?

FREDERIC
I am within my rights.

OCTAVIUS
Which no one disputes.
Though your own change of heart does somewhat refute.
You once loved the defendant. Bear this in mind.
Now you hate him enough to repay him in kind?

FREDERIC
I have a duty.

OCTAVIUS
And where is it, duty ends?
With you an executioner, transformed by revenge?

FREDERIC
Bring him.

(OCTAVIUS leads BERNARD forward, removes the prisoner's blindfold, but not the chains around his wrists.)

BERNARD
You won't get away with this. I know the law.

FREDERIC
Be careful, Sir, what conclusions you draw.
I am judge of this town, and the power is mine
To arrest, interrogate and to confine.

BERNARD
I know what you're after. I know this game!
It's Constance you want, so you slander my name
With false accusation and public arrest!

FREDERIC
Justice is my duty. Truth alone is my quest.

BERNARD
Your quest is my betrothed, my money and lands.
Sir Justice Rat! These are your plans!

FREDERIC
Address me as Your Honor.

BERNARD
      Honorable bastard, I say!

OCTAVIUS
He wants manners.

FREDERIC
   And respect. Take him away.
A month in the dungeon may make him more polite.

BERNARD
No, wait. Very well. Ask what questions you might.
But I protest, and I answer under duress.

OCTAVIUS
Stand straight. Face the judge. Answer clearly, "yes"
Or "no."

FREDERIC
   You once had a wife. Is this not true?

BERNARD
Ah. Now I see what you are trying to do.
An enemy has filled your ears with some lie—

FREDERIC
You were married. Do you confirm or deny?

BERNARD
I am a widower. Reason it out on your own.

OCTAVIUS
You will answer the question.

BERNARD
Leave me alone!

FREDERIC
What have you done with her?

BERNARD
Done with whom?

FREDERIC
Your late wife.

BERNARD
I placed her in a tomb.

FREDERIC
And where is it, this tomb? Show it to me.

BERNARD
You'll have to swim—the bottom of the sea.

FREDERIC
Your wife drowned at sea. Is this what you claim?

BERNARD
I do not. But she's dead. So it's all the same.

FREDERIC
Tell the court, what was the cause of her death?

BERNARD
Too little heartbeat, not enough breath.

FREDERIC
I begin to lose my patience. You stand accused—

BERNARD
No, Sir Lawless Judge, I stand here abused!

FREDERIC
You will stand till you drop, or answer the charge!
The matter is grave. The stakes here are large.
If you value your freedom, if you value your life,
Answer! You are charged with the murder of your wife.

BERNARD
I demand to be let go!

FREDERIC
                     Through cunning and guile
You led your loving wife to a deserted isle.
Without food or drink, to the elements exposed,
You left her to die, then returned here and chose
A new wife, more to your taste.

BERNARD
                            No! This I deny!

FREDERIC
I know what you have done. I do not yet know why.

BERNARD
What evidence do you have? Show me—what proof?

FREDERIC
A witness, who knows all, and who speaks the truth.

BERNARD
Bring him forth. Let me face him, now, right here!

FREDERIC
In good time. The prospect fills you with fear.

BERNARD
I fear that I am slandered, a victim of lies.

FREDERIC
You, a victim?

BERNARD
    No man who knows me denies
I loved my wife. Too often, was I criticized
For the doting affection that I could not hide.
Jealous women would say Julie had me bewitched.
I would sit at her feet, and stare, transfixed,
At her beauty, unmatched in all of France.
They spoke true. I was indeed entranced.
Looking in her eyes, I'd see her very soul.
Her love redeemed me and made me whole.
My joy, my existence was at its height.
  (A beat. He cannot go on.)

FREDERIC
And then?

BERNARD
    And then, ceaseless night
Descended. And I with it.

FREDERIC
Why? What came to pass?

BERNARD
I cannot—

FREDERIC
Tell me.

BERNARD
She breathed her last.

FREDERIC
The reason!

BERNARD
The reason...

FREDERIC
Confess! Tell me why!

BERNARD
Illness—

FREDERIC
You murdered her—

BERNARD
That's a lie—

FREDERIC
Men! Driven always by desire and greed!
Create a Garden of Eden; they contribute weed.

No perfection on earth they would not destroy.
Was ever creature born less deserving of joy?

BERNARD
You wrong me to think I alone am to blame—

FREDERIC
O! Hopeless fool! that ever wished this exchange!
Constance for Julie? Tallow wax for gold!

BERNARD
That was never my wish—

FREDERIC
                Your refrain grows old.
I heard remorse in your words—or so I believed.
But justice will not be so easily deceived.
The charge against you stands. Do you confess?

BERNARD
To acting as a man—no more and no less.

FREDERIC
So be it. You were given your chance.
Now in accordance with the law of these lands,
I proclaim the defendant suspected by me
Of withholding the truth. Therefore, this remedy:
Be he stretched, this day, for one hour's time
Upon the rack, until he confess his crime.

OCTAVIUS
Your Honor, I beg you—

BERNARD
What madness is this?

FREDERIC
Not madness, but justice, which you shall not resist.
Lead the defendant away.

BERNARD
Hear me, first!
I have the answer you want. At home, in my purse.
One thousand ducats. They belong, Sir, to you.
In exchange for my freedom.

FREDERIC
This I cannot do.
Take him out.

BERNARD
Not enough? I give you more.
One thousand ducats now become four.
Sir! I know the object that most you prize.
Take Constance! She's yours! Make her your bride!
I give her to you.

FREDERIC
She's not yours to bestow.
Even were she, to your offer I would answer, No.

BERNARD
Whence this hatred for me? I beg you! Please!
Show me some mercy. Must I get on my knees?
   (Falls to his knees.)

FREDERIC
She begged you once thus. What mercy did you show?
Do you hope to reap what you failed to sow?

BERNARD
No! What must I do?

FREDERIC
One thing only: Confess.
Did you kill your wife? Answer me!
(A beat.)

BERNARD
Yes.

FREDERIC
Octavius.

OCTAVIUS
Sir?

FREDERIC
Remove this man's chain.

(He does so.)

FREDERIC
Now leave us, Octavius.

OCTAVIUS
Sir, I should remain—

FREDERIC
Fear him not. My moment at last draws near.

OCTAVIUS
You play your part too well. It is you I fear.
(Exit OCTAVIUS.)

SCENE TWO

FREDERIC
Arise and face me. We are now alone.
Life or death is the choice. This time, your own.
If you now confess all, you may yet live.
Resist, and no such hope can I give.

BERNARD
Hear me, Your Honor—

FREDERIC
                    Be truthful in your reply.
I know what you have done. Now tell me why.

BERNARD
To argue my innocence, I ask nothing more.
Yes, I left my wife upon that hateful shore.
But there are reasons, Your Honor, for my act.

FREDERIC
Now would I hear them—supported by fact.

BERNARD
My seeming desperation, this you'll understand,
When in confidence I tell you, man to man—

I now speak the word I am loathe to hear,
That damns the very soul of the woman I held dear,
That of himself, no man hopes ever be said:
Cuckold.

FREDERIC
Cuckold!?

BERNARD
My wife dishonored my bed.

FREDERIC
She did *what—!?*

BERNARD
She stained it with her lust.

FREDERIC
Liar! Your fiction fills me with disgust!

BERNARD
The punishment was harsh. I admit, this is true.
And yet, I did what I had legal right to do.
A wife's infidelity is remedied by our laws.
A husband is protected—

FREDERIC
If there is cause.
Where is your evidence? Furnish me with proof.

BERNARD
All who know me, know I speak only the truth.

FREDERIC
Yet, the same is said of Julie. All who knew her
Declare no woman more faithful, none who was truer,
Nor more honest, they say, nor ever so chaste.
On every tongue, her name is still praised,
Save by you. Tell me: How can this be?

BERNARD
'Twas I alone who knew of her duplicity.

FREDERIC
So. A husband, wronged.

BERNARD
                    Imagine what I went through.
In the victim's role, place yourself.

FREDERIC
                    Oh, yes. I do.

BERNARD
The shame I felt. My utter humiliation.
Think where this all took place—

FREDERIC
                    In your imagination.

BERNARD
You refuse to take my charges seriously?

FREDERIC
Not one is based on evidence, from what I can see.
Suspicion of a woman's imprudent act:

This the source of your furious wrath?
In your judgment, Bernard, how merciless you are.
Every day honest people commit worse acts, by far.
If adulterers were punished with such cruel exile,
This city would be as empty as that desert isle.

BERNARD

A question of honor. I love honor more than life.

FREDERIC

To your shame, you loved honor more than your wife.
Return to your charge against the virtuous Julie:
Let us now suppose, even if you speak truly,
That you confronted her. How did she respond
When you told her you knew of this scandalous wrong?

BERNARD

I never did so.

FREDERIC
How is that? Not a word?

BERNARD

I thought it better to wait, and see what occurred.

FREDERIC

Cleverly you waited, to catch them both in the act?

BERNARD

Yes, that's it.

FREDERIC

Then you're free. Simply give me this fact.
His name.

BERNARD
His name?

FREDERIC
Her lover, whom you surprised.

BERNARD
I—I can't.

FREDERIC
Just as I thought.

BERNARD
He was in disguise.

FREDERIC
What!?

BERNARD
He took care to hide his face,
And so protect himself from public disgrace.

FREDERIC
Surely, of your wife, you demanded his name.

BERNARD
No.

FREDERIC
And why not, man!?

BERNARD
Out of shame.

FREDERIC
Shame, you say?

BERNARD
This town is my home.
Where I live and shall die. Here I am known
As an honest man. I have the people's respect.
I hid my disgrace, so that none should suspect
Her betrayal.

FREDERIC
Yes, none. Not even she.

BERNARD
She was guilty—

FREDERIC
So say you!

BERNARD
—of adultery.

FREDERIC
Tried by the victim, with no chance to reply!
By her accuser, in secret, sentenced to die!
Tell me, where is honor and justice in *this?*

BERNARD
The justice is hers. The honor is his.

FREDERIC
Your word against hers. She can't answer the charge.
I answer in her place, and I accuse Bernard

Of murder. Now, Defendant, mark me well,
Or accept the alternative: your place in hell.
Bring me the man who was with her that night.
Failing that, a witness, credible, who did sight
Them both, together locked in illicit embrace,
To swear publicly before God what took place.
All appeals to clemency I do hereby reject.
Obey, or at dawn you will hang by the neck.
  (Exit FREDERIC.)

END OF ACT FOUR

ACT FIVE

SCENE ONE

(DON LOPE, practicing his expert swordplay; flexing, sharpening, cleaning, etc., his collection of weapons. CONSTANCE, making an effort not to appear impressed, observes.)

CONSTANCE
You're not bad at that.

DON LOPE
I am a deadly force.

CONSTANCE
In war, or conversation?

DON LOPE
You mock me, of course.

CONSTANCE
I, mock you? Sir, what gives you that impression?

DON LOPE
Laugh while you can. I have in my possession
Certain means to take that smirk off your face.

CONSTANCE
So. The brave soldier will put me in my place?

DON LOPE
For that very task, Madam, I have been bred.

CONSTANCE
And where *is* my place?

DON LOPE
On your back, in my bed.

CONSTANCE
You will win *that* battle, Captain, only in your dreams.
I am free to choose my lover.

DON LOPE
To you, so it seems.
I have set myself a goal. I plan to succeed.
I intend to tame you. It is discipline you need.

CONSTANCE
The boasting soldier. Really, Sir. You bore me.
All these swaggering tales and Spanish vainglory.
You're a champion swordsman. I grant you, that's true.
Yet, of all your admirers, the foremost ... is you.

DON LOPE
You accuse me of vanity and pride. Is that it?

CONSTANCE
Oh, you're sharp, Don Lope. What rapier wit.

DON LOPE
Your insults do not harm me. These I rise above.
And I counterattack by reasserting my love.

CONSTANCE
Ha! You're relentless. You refuse to understand?
Let me spell it out: You're not my kind of man.
Your favor and attentions, these I reject.
Is that clear?

DON LOPE
Yes. But this I cannot accept.

CONSTANCE
Good God...

DON LOPE
You underestimate the military spirit.
This attempt to dissuade me— No, no, I won't hear it.
Unconditional surrender—this is your fate.
With my weapon unsheathed, I stand at your gate.

CONSTANCE
Well, re-sheath it, please, and leave me alone.

DON LOPE
No negotiations. Madam, let it be known
That you are my target, my trophy of war,
Or I am not Don Lope, conquistador!

CONSTANCE
He's mad. He's mad. He hears nothing I say.

DON LOPE
Once we are married, I shall take you away.
France is full of Frenchmen, which I cannot abide.
We'll to Spain.

CONSTANCE
Not this girl.

DON LOPE
I shall decide.

CONSTANCE
Captain, give up. You shall not win this heart.

DON LOPE
I am determined as a rock.

CONSTANCE
And just as smart.
I have plans, Don Lope, and they don't include you.
With my life, I alone shall decide what to do.

DON LOPE
Tell me, proud Constance, what your plans entail.
Are you looking forward to a wedding in jail?

CONSTANCE
Jail? What is this, conquistador humor?

DON LOPE
You yourself are free to confirm the rumor.
Of your three suitors, there is now one less.
Bernard has been placed, it seems, under arrest.

CONSTANCE
What?

DON LOPE
The murder of his wife is the charge.

Not the ideal husband, hot-tempered Bernard.
At this moment, he sits, a prisoner in chains.

(A beat. CONSTANCE giggles.)

DON LOPE
Impressive, my dear, how you mask your pain.

CONSTANCE
Bernard, charged with murder. Of course, don't you see?
Frederic has acted—he's done it for me!
His rival for my hand, now utterly defeated.

DON LOPE
By law, not by sword. I say he cheated.

CONSTANCE
You're jealous—and worried. I shall have the last laugh.
Cross swords with Freddie, he'll slice you in half.

DON LOPE *(laughing)*.
Spare me such jesting, I beg of you, please.
Your "Freddie," with his sword, couldn't slice cheese.

(DON LOPE now advances on CONSTANCE.)

CONSTANCE
Slanderer! Very soon, you'll learn your lesson,
When Frederic recoiffes your hair with his weapon!
First one ear, then the next. Your knees grow weak,
As he coolly carves his name in your cheek.
Count yourself lucky to escape with your life—

(DON LOPE takes her in an embrace.)

DON LOPE

Constance. Accept it. You shall be my wife.
Say the word and we marry within the hour.
I can sense your desire. You can feel my power.

CONSTANCE *(escaping him)*.

My flame burns for Frederic; for you, I have none.
Don Lope. Accept it. The better man has won.

DON LOPE

Has he? I fear that you are wrong.

CONSTANCE

Sir, I don't wish to see your pain prolonged.
It is hopeless. Forget me. I've made my decision.

DON LOPE

Your plans, my dear, may need some revision.
Frederic and I have had a conversation.
He expressed—how shall I say?—some reservation
About marrying you, or anyone else.
The great flaw in your plan is Frederic himself.

CONSTANCE

You're lying. What loathsome slander is this?

DON LOPE

He swore to me that you would never be his.
No, nature to Frederick was cruelly detrimental.
Heaven denied him something essential.
I am a connoisseur, Madam, of masculinity,
And I tell you, he lacks the proper... machinery.
In plain words, Madam, so you will understand:
I think your Frederic's more woman than man.

CONSTANCE
Oh! You vile offender of my innocent ears!

DON LOPE
I only mean to say, there are men, and there are queers.

CONSTANCE
Stop! I won't listen!

DON LOPE
    The fact remains, still.
For marriage, Frederic lacks both power and will.

CONSTANCE
He is refined, and fashionable, a lover of verse.

DON LOPE
Let us hope, for your sake, he loves nothing worse.

CONSTANCE
O! That Frederic were here, to answer your lies!

(Enter FREDERIC.)

SCENE TWO

DON LOPE
Ah, the man himself: what a pleasant surprise.

CONSTANCE *(runs to FREDERIC).*
Frederic! Darling! At last, you're here.
This despicable soldier has filled my ear
With filth and insult and outrageous claim.

He attacks your manhood, impugns your good name.
Defend yourself, Frederic—and me.

DON LOPE
>Yes. Do.

CONSTANCE
Peel this man like a mango. Run him through.

FREDERIC
Before we fill the streets with the dead,
Might I know a bit more about what he said?

CONSTANCE
Bernard you arrested, and placed in chains.

FREDERIC
Quite true.

CONSTANCE
>And well done. But then he claims,
Though you boldly defeat the rival for my hand,
There is reason to think you less than a man.

FREDERIC
Quite true.

CONSTANCE
>Dear, this is no time for false modesty.
You're a victim of the cruelest calumny.
Hear now this scoundrel's vile invention:
That to marry me now is not your intention.

FREDERIC
Quite true.

CONSTANCE *(to DON LOPE)*.
There, you see?
(Double-take.) What!?

FREDERIC
Let me explain.

DON LOPE
Constance, this would never happen in Spain.

CONSTANCE
This is some nightmare, some cowardly trick—

FREDERIC
Hear my reasons—

CONSTANCE
Oh, I think I'm going to be sick...

FREDERIC
You begged me to rescue you from Bernard.
Your freedom I give you. I cannot give my heart.
I acknowledge your attractions. They are widely known.

DON LOPE
Caution...

FREDERIC
In fact, they are much like my own.

DON LOPE *(to CONSTANCE).*
I told you.

FREDERIC
Never did I wish to cause you pain.

CONSTANCE
Nor soil my reputation with this mark of shame?
In love, my affection has always been returned.
Never, but never has my love been spurned.
And my lovers are legion. If only you knew.

DON LOPE
Legion? How many?

CONSTANCE
Well. Not "legion." A few.

FREDERIC
You are angry and wounded. Lady, I sympathize—

CONSTANCE
By every man of this town, I am considered a prize.
You professed a "desire." A wonder what *this* meant?
Don Lope was right. You lack the equipment.
Oh, the shame of it, Frederic, the indignity.
How, how, how could you do this to me?

FREDERIC
Dear Constance. The reasons are many and varied.

CONSTANCE
Oh!

FREDERIC
But the foremost is ... I'm already married.

CONSTANCE
What!?

DON LOPE
What!?

FREDERIC
I admit, this may come as a shock.

DON LOPE
Scoundrel!

CONSTANCE
Polygamist!

FREDERIC
If you'll just let me talk—

CONSTANCE
And cover me further with filth and disgrace?

DON LOPE
Madam, I stand ready to rearrange his face.

FREDERIC
Remember, please, I made no formal vow—

CONSTANCE
What does that make me, then? Some cow?
Pleased to mate "informally" in some field?

FREDERIC
You mistake me—

CONSTANCE
True Frederic is now revealed.
Ah, men! Their hearts, ever governed by lust.
In woman's name, I ask of God: Is this just?

DON LOPE
No!

CONSTANCE
Don Lope. There is but one thing to do.

DON LOPE
Madam.

CONSTANCE
Slice him like a sausage. Run him through.

DON LOPE
My pleasure.

FREDERIC
Constance, let us not act in haste—

CONSTANCE
I act in revenge, Sir. I am in disgrace.

FREDERIC
Bloodshed is something we can ill afford.
I am a judge—

Act V LOVERS AND EXECUTIONERS

DON LOPE
Your Honor: Choose your sword.

FREDERIC
Oh, not again...

DON LOPE
You find the prospect upsetting?
Think of it medically: an impromptu bloodletting.

(DON LOPE tosses FREDERIC a sword. Swordplay.)

FREDERIC
This is madness, I tell you. A gross exaggeration—!

DON LOPE
What bodily part receives the first laceration?
The shoulder? The ribs?

CONSTANCE
I prefer the thigh.

DON LOPE
Very good, my dear. I readily comply.

FREDERIC
Swords are unlawful!

DON LOPE
By what law? Can you name it?

FREDERIC
Better yet, as a judge, I hereby proclaim it!

(Swordplay.)

FREDERIC
Caution, Don Lope. You shall provoke my wrath.

CONSTANCE
Did he say "provoke"?

DON LOPE
    We cannot but laugh.

(CONSTANCE and DON LOPE laugh.)

FREDERIC
To your sense of compassion, Constance, I appeal.

DON LOPE
I answer for the lady with this: cold steel.

(Swordplay.)

CONSTANCE
Oh, Don! Well done!

DON LOPE
    In that move, I am a leader.
My ripostes have been likened to surgical procedure.

CONSTANCE
What *was* that move?

DON LOPE
    Madam, with bravado,
A fully-extended, left-lead passado.

CONSTANCE
May we see that again? What a thing of beauty.

DON LOPE
Madam, to thrill you, I consider it my duty.

FREDERIC
All fighting must stop. Cease and desist!

CONSTANCE *(to FREDERIC).*
Look, do you mind?

DON LOPE
The proper movement is this.
(DON LOPE demonstrates a passado.)

CONSTANCE
Oh, that's exquisite.

DON LOPE
Yes, is it not?

CONSTANCE
Marvelous "passado"!

DON LOPE
Although, I think I'll slay him with a classic staccado.
That is, my dear, if it meets with your approval.

CONSTANCE
You are an artist, Don. Proceed with his removal.

DON LOPE *(bowing).*
Your humble servant.

(FREDERIC seizes the moment and slashes DON LOPE across the buttocks.)

CONSTANCE
Oh!

DON LOPE
I have been attacked.

CONSTANCE
You vile assassin!

FREDERIC
I'm sorry— Look, it's only a scratch—

DON LOPE
Big, big mistake. Oh, *very* big. Señor:
You have cut the sacred flesh of a conquistador.
En garde, corpse.

(Vigorous attack by DON LOPE; effective retreating defense by FREDERIC. At last, FREDERIC is disarmed and pinned.)

FREDERIC
Have mercy. Stay your hand.

DON LOPE
You fight like a woman. Now die like a man.

FREDERIC
Constance. Call him off. Is your heart made of stone?

Act V   LOVERS AND EXECUTIONERS

CONSTANCE
I answer with the sign of ancient Rome.

(CONSTANCE gives a "thumb-down" sign, then joins DON LOPE.)

FREDERIC
Can love to murder so quickly turn?

CONSTANCE
My honor you murdered. My revenge you earn.

FREDERIC
Wait! One word more!

DON LOPE
Your last, it shall be.

FREDERIC
Your honors can't be wounded by one such as me.
I, married to Constance—nature would object!

CONSTANCE
Groveling upsets me.

DON LOPE
Yes. Have some respect.
Stand tall, false lover. Prepare your soul to depart.
Takes this blow, unmanly Frederic, direct to the heart.

(DON LOPE, his sword raised, places his hand on FREDERIC's heart—or in this case, breast. DON LOPE's hand freezes. Double-take. He drops his sword, rips open FREDERIC's shirt, then instantly closes it again.)

DON LOPE.

Madre de Dios...

CONSTANCE
Oh my God...

DON LOPE
Is this some jest?

FREDERIC
I take it seriously, Sir. This is my breast.

CONSTANCE
That face. That voice... Are you woman or ghost?

FREDERIC
Both, Madam, too nearly. My God, that was close.
(Removes her disguise.)

CONSTANCE
Unless this be sorcery, I can scarce believe my eyes.
Frederic was never Frederic, but Julie, in disguise.

DON LOPE

Who?

CONSTANCE
Bernard's wife.

DON LOPE
The one he murdered.

CONSTANCE
I think not.
Julie? Is it you?

JULIE
So it is.

CONSTANCE
Oh, devilish plot!

DON LOPE
You are a wizard, Madam, some spirit or witch.

CONSTANCE
In my opinion, she's an incomparable bitch!
Courting me in disguise— I am made to look a clown.

DON LOPE
And I, wounded by a woman. I shall never live it down.

CONSTANCE
Impersonating a judge, as well. Have you lost your head?
Such tasteless behavior. You're supposed to be dead.

JULIE
For escaping death, I show a talent quite rare.
Forgive me, both. I know it seems unfair
To be treated thus. I employed my disguise
With good reason: to forestall my own demise.
One thing I came to learn; I seek to learn it still:
Why my husband Bernard wished to have me killed.

DON LOPE
Judging from your actions, I can hazard a guess.

JULIE

Let me try, with my reasons, to make your anger less.
Hear then my plans, for I would count upon your aid,
As I approach the end of this strange masquerade.
And Constance, be not dismayed, a suitor to have lost.
My replacement, I warrant, is well worth the cost.
Follow me now, I pray you, and let me explain.

(CONSTANCE and DON LOPE exchange glances.)

CONSTANCE

This better be good.

DON LOPE

This would *not* happen in Spain.

(They exit, as lights fade, then rise on BERNARD.)

SCENE THREE

(BERNARD, a prisoner, awaiting trial.)

BERNARD

This moment I have dreaded for three long years.
Topic of my dreams, source of all my fears.
I am discovered, unmasked, trapped in the snare
That I myself laid. Here at last is despair.
Now must I produce, to save my own life,
Proof that I was betrayed by my own wife.
It was this, above all, I had hoped to evade.
Now am I a fool and a prisoner made.
Oh, she haunts me still. Her ghost is nigh.

I feel her! I hear her vengeful cry,
Trumpeting my doom!

(GUZMAN has entered, with wood and tools. He blows his nose, producing a loud honk.)

BERNARD
Guzman! Come to set me free!

GUZMAN
Well, to tell you the truth, Sir, actually ...
I'm here for other reasons. Some light construction.
To soften the blow, Sir, of my salary reduction.

BERNARD
What reduction? What are you talking about?
I am sentenced to die!

GUZMAN
Sir, there's no need to shout.
The mess that you're in, I truly deplore.
But seeing as you won't be around anymore—

BERNARD
Not around? Why you traitor—!

GUZMAN
Now, Sir, don't be rash.
An odd job, that's all, for a little extra cash.

BERNARD
I need your help!

GUZMAN
That may have to wait,
Till I finish the gallows.

BERNARD
Gallows!? That will be too late!

GUZMAN
At *my* pace, Sir, death will not quickly come.
Relax. Nothing to hang you on till I'm done.
   (Arranging his wood.)
Now how should this go? One here, one there...
I thought, something nice, with railing and stair.

BERNARD
You idiot!

GUZMAN
All right. So the stairs, we lose.

BERNARD
In a matter of hours, my neck is in a noose!

GUZMAN
So keep the stairs. It seems rather odd, then.
After all, once you're dead, what's the problem?

BERNARD
God help me...

GUZMAN
Incidentally, I would like it known,
I dig excellent graves, Sir. *And* I carve stone.

You could have the prettiest gravesite in France.
Though from you I must ask payment in advance.

BERNARD
Guzman. Help me. There is yet some hope.
I may manage still to avoid the rope.

GUZMAN
I'm not in charge of rope, Sir. Just the carpentry.
But wait. Will I be paid, if you're set free?

BERNARD
Was I not a good master? Generous and kind?

GUZMAN
Well, let me think... No, nothing comes to mind.

BERNARD
Through good times and bad, I kept you employed.

GUZMAN
Your boot to my backside, I worked to avoid.

BERNARD
I trusted you. Partly. Even though you cheat me.

GUZMAN
And I could trust *you* most days to beat me.

BERNARD
I gave clothes, and shelter. And healthful food.

GUZMAN
Rags, a leaky roof, and chicken bones half-chewed.

BERNARD
Ingrate! Without me, you'd have begged in the street!
And incidentally, those bones had a good deal of meat.

GUZMAN
I've been with you a while, Sir. I can honestly say,
After you're hanged, I'll miss you—in a way.

BERNARD
Hanging! Oh, merciful God, I'm afraid...

GUZMAN
Look at the bright side: It's faster than the plague.
Though painful, and violent. Messy too, so it's said.
But once it's all over, Sir— Hey, you're dead.

BERNARD
Guzman. I need Beatrice. If she'll tell what she saw,
I may yet escape the full force of the law.
Find her, I beg you. Run, Guzman. Fly!
She is my witness, my sole alibi.

GUZMAN
Sir, we go back a long way, you and me.
So I'll help you, of course—for a modest fee.

BERNARD *(digging in his pockets).*
I have two ducats. Three. Surely, that's enough.

GUZMAN
The truth of the matter is, times are tough.

BERNARD
Here's four, you thief! In the name of God, go!

GUZMAN
Sir, I shall—though I expect the pace will be slow.
Never did four ducats purchase much speed.
Five's a swift number—

BERNARD
A curse on your greed!

GUZMAN
Sir, let's not argue over one tiny ducat.
What will it matter, once you kick the bucket?

(BERNARD tosses GUZMAN another coin.)

BERNARD
Get out of my sight!

GUZMAN
Oh, and, Sir? While I'm gone?
Could you maybe get a bit of the gallows-work done?

BERNARD
Go! *(Exit GUZMAN, swiftly. A beat.)*
   Damn the abominable mess I am in!
Trusting scoundrels and servants to save my skin.
Oh, Fate: One drop of pity is my only request.
There's some justice in my suffering—but not in my death.

SCENE FOUR

(BEATRICE, alone. She approaches the place where BERNARD is being held.)

BEATRICE

Why, pray tell, are they called the "well-to-do"?
They do nothing well, that I ever knew.
Can they cook, or milk, or mend a pair of breeches?
No. But at moans, wails, cries and screeches,
They're virtuosos, dancing gaily their special ballet
Of condemning the lady's-maid and blaming the valet
For every crisis or quandary or incidence of gas.
Yet did *I* gluttonize? Or choose those shoes? Need you ask?
Great duelers and feuders and slingers of mud,
Playing at swords and spilling each other's blood.
Stick them all in a room, close the door, turn the key:
You'd have a carnival of skull-splitting butchery.
Pity, then, the rich. There's this defect in wealth:
It's a pestilent, plagueful corruption of health.
Money's a terrible source of fevers and dreams.
Oh, the night-sweats pour out of the rich in streams.
The eyes hyper-dilatate. The nervous twitch begins.
Aggrandizement of the waist. Doubling of the chins.
The back humpifies. The spine will curve and twist.
There's the tightening, arthritical effect upon the fist.
Worse—worse by far—is the pressure on the brain.
They begin to pontificate, propound and proclaim.
Words like "honor" and "justice" escape through their teeth,
As if they'd become the Oracle of ancient Greece.
Oh, the suffering souls. To help them is our task,
We the high-minded members of the lower class.
Someone must reach out to them, again and again.
If not us, who? If not now, when?

Act V   LOVERS AND EXECUTIONERS   131

After all, I ask you: What is a lower class for?
To make the rich less rich, the poor less poor.
I am summoned now to jail. I graciously comply.
Bernard begs an audience, yet will not tell why.
Another rich man in peril. He has my sympathy.
I go to him. For surely, there's something in it for me.
   (She takes a step to leave, stops.)
But soft. Comes this nettlesome thought to me:
Where justice does strike, I would rather not be.
Jail leads to court. Court leads to law,
Whose long arm ends in the lion's paw.
The law is a prodigious digger of graves,
Filled not with the rich, but ever with knaves.
All talk of justice does fearfully affect us.
The question is, From justice, who shall protect us?
The prisoner summons Beatrice? Beatrice smells a rat.
Questions and answers. No, I'll have none of that.
Innocent is a most approximate term.
And justice, too often the proverbial worm,
Gnaws at the truth till it gets full inside.
And each of us, in truth, has something to hide.
Ought the humble crow be expected to sing?
It's outside her talent. Instead, she takes wing.

   (BEATRICE turns to flee, but runs straight into GUZ-
   MAN, who has entered silently from behind during the
   last few lines of her speech. GUZMAN spins her around
   and heads her back into position for the next scene.)

SCENE FIVE

(Where BERNARD is being held. A patch of light, ringed by shadow.)

BERNARD
Beatrice. At last.

BEATRICE
Sir, you don't look well.

BERNARD
Nor should I. I stand at the gates of hell.
My life is in danger. With murder, I am charged.

BEATRICE
Why, this is scarcely credible. A murderer? Bernard?

BERNARD
Soon I shall swing from the end of a rope,
But you shall help me, Beatrice. You're my last hope.

(BERNARD begins to stalk BEATRICE, who retreats, while trying not to reveal how frightened she is.)

BEATRICE
To serve is my calling, Sir. There I'm born and bred.
And besides, there's no profit in serving the dead.
A message to my mistress? Is that your desire?
In your moment of distress, you wish to sit by her,
And draw strength from her beauty. Now that's romantic.
If she knew of your state, she'd be possibly frantic.

BERNARD
Constance has no remedy to my present despair.
For all but you, Woman, it is beyond repair.

BEATRICE
I, Sir? But how?

BERNARD
You need only speak true.

BEATRICE
Though true speaking be rare, it's an art I can do.

BERNARD
You shall be well rewarded. That's a promise I make.

BEATRICE
What do I care for money, Sir? Your life is at stake.
No money, but compassion. No ducats, but tears.
Let not "money" foul your tongue, nor infect my ears.
To serve you unselfishly, before heaven and earth.
Why, who could imagine what such service is worth?
Ten ducats? Twenty? The mind boggles at the thought.
What price, a life, Sir?

BERNARD
The answer?

BEATRICE
A lot.
But talk not of money. What truth must I declare?

BERNARD
That you were a witness. That you were there.
You saw her lover flee. You need only say this.

BEATRICE
You forbade me, Sir, warning my life would be at risk.
At my throat, I remember the feel of your blade.
I would die, said you, if your secret I betrayed.

BERNARD
Listen to me: from this pledge, you are released.

BEATRICE
But, Sir, your shame—

BERNARD
                Better shamed than deceased.
A man may be cuckold many times in this life,
But hanged only once for the murder of his wife.
Under oath, by you, these words must be said:
Julie betrayed Bernard. She dishonored his bed.

BEATRICE
Under oath, Sir?

BERNARD
                Before the judge, you must swear.

BEATRICE
Unto God?

BERNARD
       Upon the Bible.

BEATRICE
    Sir, I—I don't dare.

BERNARD
What, foolish woman!?

BEATRICE
    Sir, to swear before the law—

BERNARD
You need only swear to the facts of what you saw!
Speak but honestly, woman, and what have you to dread?

BEATRICE
Sir, to swear an oath, and speak ill of the dead—
The truth, Sir, is slippery. What if some small lie
Invaded the words with which I testify?
My soul to the fires of hell will be damned—

BERNARD
Fear God if you must, but fear also this hand.
  (BERNARD grabs her.)

BEATRICE
I fear you, Sir, and the law, in kind,
But perjury, Sir—that's a hanging crime.

BERNARD
If this be some act, you do push me too far.
Will you bargain for terms? Tell me what they are.
But say now, you witch, how you will be bought!
Sell me now my life!

BEATRICE
Sir, I cannot.

BERNARD
Devil, from what corner of hell did you crawl!?
You will speak the truth, or never speak at all!

(BERNARD has her by the throat. During the past few moments, several figures have approached silently from different directions. In the shadows, they form a wide ring around BERNARD. A gallows now appears, with steps leading up to the scaffold where the noose swings. When FREDERIC speaks, the lights rise.)

FREDERIC
Defendant, face the court. Let your trial commence.

SCENE SIX

(BERNARD's trial. FREDERIC, dressed in judicial clothing, presides. Observing are CONSTANCE, DON LOPE, GUZMAN, and OCTAVIUS. BEATRICE takes her place among the observers. BERNARD stands alone, center stage.)

FREDERIC
Murder is the charge. Answer now in your defense,
Before the citizens of this town, your fellows and peers.

BERNARD
Your Honor, I beg you, I am not as it appears.

FREDERIC
You're a man of violent temper. Do you this deny?

BERNARD
When wronged, a man takes action, or must try.

FREDERIC
And might murder be a part of this manly attempt?

BERNARD
Sir, yes. Or no, not murder, death is what I meant—

FREDERIC
To your wife's demise, you have freely confessed.
Is this not so?

BERNARD
Your Honor—

FREDERIC
Is it not?

BERNARD
Yes.

FREDERIC
Upon an unpeopled island, by you she was left,
Exposed to the elements, to await her own death.

BERNARD
She died by my hand. This I do not contest.
My misery o'er it is great. Yet my guilt is less.

FREDERIC
Guilty, and yet not? Sir, you reason too fine.

BERNARD
Neither guilt nor disgrace, here alone is mine.

DON LOPE
Give, Sir, your reasons.

BERNARD
               Of circumstance I spoke.
'Tis true, I persuaded her upon that boat,
Then heartless abandoned her upon that shore.
Yet for me Julie died a full month before,
And my former self with her. Know then my shame:
She dishonored my bed. She abased my good name.

CONSTANCE
Was Julie not so righteous as to us she seemed?

BERNARD
By this her betrayal are my actions redeemed—
If it please Your Honor.

FREDERIC
              Please me it does not.
Proof of her deception must still be sought.
Adulteress, say you, Sir. If this brand she did earn,
Bring forth a witness, your charge to confirm.

BERNARD
Here's one, Your Honor, whose word will be believed.
She was present the night that I was deceived.

(BERNARD grabs BEATRICE, pulls her center stage.)

FREDERIC
Let her speak, under oath to her God and king.
Beatrice. Against Julie, what evidence do you bring?

BEATRICE
Good Your Honor, the wrath of law I do dread.
Even more, Sir, I fear the revenge of the dead.
To relive that moment, no, my heart does refuse.
I lack courage, Your Honor, and wish to be excused.

FREDERIC
Of all you know, Woman, you shall make us aware,
Or the anger of this court will be yours to bear.
You were Julie's maidservant, with her night and day.
Is this not true?

BEATRICE
Sir, it is just as you say.

FREDERIC
You were witness to her moods, her thought and desire.
What was her character?

BEATRICE
Sir, only to admire.
She had a ready heart, and treated all with good will.

BERNARD
Too ready, her husband's empty bed to fill.

FREDERIC
Spoke she ill of her husband, beyond his ear?

BEATRICE
Never, Your Honor. She held him always most dear.
She nurtured the good in him. A kiss and a laugh
Would transform him. She was all his better half.

BERNARD
This I do not contest. Yet there remains the fact,
Of her damning, illegal, adulterous act.
I sheltered and clothed her, fed her and prayed
For her soul. In return, I was betrayed.
Let justice think on this. It bears reflection.
My own life ended, when I uncovered her deception.

BEATRICE
Oh, pity, Sir, please! How deceived you are still!

FREDERIC
The demand of the law remains to fulfill.
Proof, Sir, proof! of your wife's adultery,
Or murderer this court will declare you to be.

DON LOPE
This goes too far.

BERNARD
              Beatrice, I charge you, speak.
The facts of her betrayal must you now repeat.

BEATRICE
Sir, I cannot.

BERNARD
      Woman, you will,
Or with your silence an innocent man you kill!

BEATRICE

If I condemn by silence, so it condemns me.
In words now, what reprieve can there be?

BERNARD

Then hear my story, all. Let Beatrice deny
What part she will, expose the slightest lie.
That cursed night, at my home I arrived.
It was moonless and dark. I knew that inside,
My wife lay sleeping. In the light of my flame,
I found the door unbolted. I thought it strange.
Silently I entered. Then, to my alarm,
A man in the shadows. I grabbed his arm.
'Twas bare. Of a sudden, he pushed me to the floor.
I leapt to my feet, but he flew out the door
Like a wild man, carrying his boots as he ran.
Into blackness he fled. Then did I understand.
You stood in the door, trembling and mute.
I declared my wife adulteress, dared you to refute.
You did not, could not. Her guilt was in your tear.
Declare now, before justice, the lie in what you hear.

BEATRICE

None, Sir.

BERNARD

Mark her.

BEATRICE

All you say is true.

BERNARD

In a bolt of revelation, I saw what I must do.
Julie's method was secrecy; so would it be mine.

To her cruel deception, I would answer in kind.
In love was I murdered, my heart slain that night.
Revenge! Who among you would deny me my right?

BEATRICE

I, Sir.

BERNARD

You? Her conspirator in this act!
We saw the lover, both. Dare you deny this fact?
Say now his name! Reveal the author of this crime!
The lover! Name him now!

BEATRICE

The lover, Sir, was mine.

BERNARD

Yours?

BEATRICE

At my throat you pressed your knife.
I dared not speak the truth. I feared for my life.

BERNARD

Your lover?

BEATRICE

The young smith from the stables. Often he came,
After dark, to see me. Am I then to blame?
That you'd kill her in revenge, how could I know?
I believed her dead at sea, these many months ago.
Your Honor...

BERNARD
Julie then was faithful?

BEATRICE
Sir, even so.

BERNARD
She took no lover?

BEATRICE
Julie loved only you.

BERNARD
Then I am hanged. Hanged for a wife too true.
No cuckold am I. Reprieved.

FREDERIC
But the cost.
Your honor is saved, and your life is lost.
Prepare now the prisoner. Bind his hands.
Let the news be published throughout these lands.
For the murder of his wife, here tried was Bernard.
I, Frederic, find the defendant guilty as charged.

BERNARD
No word in my defense? Is there nothing to be said?

FREDERIC
Only this: I sentence you to hang until dead.

CONSTANCE
Your Honor, no. Some mercy is my plea.

DON LOPE
And mine. Show this man some leniency.

CONSTANCE
He has suffered, surely, for the wrong he has done.

FREDERIC
Mercy for the murderer? No. There can be none.
Justice must act in the victim's name.
A victim now in turn justice does claim.

DON LOPE
Is this not retaliation?

CONSTANCE
An eye for an eye?

FREDERIC
Men created this law, and this law I must apply.

BEATRICE
I, Sir, too, for mercy do appeal.
Though he threatened my life, yet I feel
My guilt in this. Must the law be so cold,
To condemn his earthly life and his mortal soul?

DON LOPE
The bounds of propriety, in revenge, you exceed.

FREDERIC
He must hang.

CONSTANCE
This goes beyond what we agreed.

BERNARD
Let no one plead for mercy. 'Tis not justified.
Julie now is dead and may never be revived.
Only she can forgive me. No hope have I in this.
Had I a life to trade, I would, for one last kiss.

(BERNARD now stands on the gallows, the noose about his neck.)

FREDERIC
Bernard, see now what price your honor did demand.
Prepare your soul for its descent. Your time is at hand.
You tremble.

BERNARD
The first chill of death I feel.
Your voice, Sir, and eyes. I know not what is real.

(The hood is placed over BERNARD's head.)

FREDERIC
Your dead wife now does exact her due.
Your life for hers. Bernard. Adieu.

(JULIE pulls the lever that opens the trap beneath BERNARD's feet. BERNARD and all the observers let out a cry as he plunges beneath the scaffold, and is hung.)

DON LOPE
Murderess!

CONSTANCE
You fiend! What have you done?

DON LOPE
Your own hanging, Woman, follows this illegal one!

FREDERIC
Justice is mine!

CONSTANCE
You've killed an innocent man!

DON LOPE
Your husband's blood is on your hands!

FREDERIC
Who mourned for Julie when *she* was killed?
Who called for punishment? Was heaven filled
With cries that *her* death be revenged?

DON LOPE
You are mad! See where your madness ends!

FREDERIC
In justice. And I am by it transformed.
So, too, Bernard—behold him now, reborn.

(OCTAVIUS has lowered BERNARD; he now pulls the hood from BERNARD's head: He is alive.)

CONSTANCE
This is witchcraft!

DON LOPE
Is this a corpse or a man?

FREDERIC
Something of both—all according to plan.

(All stare in amazement as BERNARD stands and surveys the group.)

BERNARD
Can this be heaven?
(Fixes on GUZMAN, who gives him a weak wave.)
No, no, it must be hell.
Are you spirits, too? Are *your* souls damned, as well?

FREDERIC
Heaven, Sir, or hell—upon ourselves that depends.

CONSTANCE
You've won. Now show mercy.

DON LOPE
And let his trial end.

FREDERIC *(removing her disguise)*.
Facing death, it is said, come visions of one's life.
Behold you now this vision.

BERNARD
God forgive me. My wife.

DON LOPE
Who yet lives.

BERNARD
She? Alive?

CONSTANCE
Sir, as you are both.

BERNARD
If not dead, I am mad, for I behold now a ghost.

DON LOPE
A spirit far too spirited.

CONSTANCE
Yet a vision to be adored.
Your wife, much forsaken, is now to you restored.

BERNARD
This soars above belief.

CONSTANCE
Rise to it, Sir. 'Tis true.

BERNARD
Will she speak?

DON LOPE
Address her.

BERNARD
Julie. Is it you?

JULIE
Much changed and resurrected, it is and is not I.

BERNARD
My judge?

DON LOPE
And executioner.

CONSTANCE
Here's "an eye for an eye"!

(GUZMAN seizes the moment to worm his way up to BERNARD.)

GUZMAN
What a pleasure, Sir, to see you looking so... undead.
In celebration, let's just forget everything I ever said.

(GUZMAN is unceremoniously pulled away by DON LOPE.)

DON LOPE
Marvel all, how heaven does arrange man's fate.
No funeral do we attend, but a wedding, celebrate.
To all this town, I announce my hard-won victory:
This young beauty does consent, Don Lope's bride to be.

CONSTANCE
Though my Captain, I do warn you: I've nothing to wear.

DON LOPE
In nothing, sweet Constance, I'll find you passing fair.
Feast with us, my friends. Help us consecrate this day.
To hope, let us drink. For redemption, let us pray.

CONSTANCE
These two we leave in private, their own way to find.
May they journey to what will, and what was, leave behind.

(DON LOPE and CONSTANCE begin to exit, accompanied by GUZMAN. BEATRICE approaches JULIE, and kneels before her.)

BEATRICE
My lady, your pardon, and my joy is complete.

JULIE
Pardons are as love. For the worthy, mine I keep.

(BEATRICE, rejected, rises and exits. OCTAVIUS remains. He goes to BERNARD.)

OCTAVIUS
In more ways than you know, Sir, you are blessed.
This your resurrection is the mirror of my death.

BERNARD
'Twas you who set the rope?

OCTAVIUS
                              And kept you alive.
For one knot less, I could have watched you die.
Good Julie, as I feared, I must now bid farewell.
Of Frederic's transformation, the Duke I shall tell.

JULIE
Loyal Octavius. Fortune was mine the day we met.
My gratitude go with you.

OCTAVIUS
                I take it, with regret.
And, Sir: If from this woman you exact more sacrifice,
I swear upon this heart, I'll make you pay the price.

(Exit OCTAVIUS. JULIE and BERNARD are now alone.)

BERNARD
My wife...

JULIE
"Husband." Bitter tastes the word.

BERNARD
To my ears now, no sweeter sound ever heard.

JULIE
Anger, as the sea, does but slowly subside.

BERNARD
Too well I know it. I was drowned in that tide.

JULIE
Revenge is a poison. Its damage yet I feel.

BERNARD
How physic this disease, Julie? How may it heal?

JULIE
How indeed, when in my blood, it does burn?
No, it's incurable. To the Duke I must return.

BERNARD
Stay, Julie. I implore you. Help me redeem
Our love. It once was worthy of esteem.

JULIE
To see it yet abused. No, I should rather live alone,
Upon that deathly isle.

BERNARD
'Tis here you have a home.

JULIE
Empty now, and haunted, by the ghosts of who we were.

BERNARD
And can be again.

JULIE
And what assurance, Sir,
That betrayal does not yet lurk behind each door?
Can trust, a thing so fragile, once broken, be restored?

BERNARD
So must it be. Or else, how may we live?

JULIE
Apart. And in regret.

BERNARD
No—if you but say the word, forgive.
(Sounds of the wedding feast can be heard, off: music, laughter, shouts. A beat.)
I envy them. Such music we once made.
Have we not as much to celebrate as they?

(Enter GUZMAN, a bit drunk.)

GUZMAN
M'Lord, m'Lady: The Spaniard bid me come
To verify if hostilities are all done
Between you. No further executions planned?
Then he bids you come, to sit at his right hand

And toast the lady author of the wound so cruel
Applied to his...self-esteem in the famous duel.

(GUZMAN bows. For the first time, JULIE allows herself a laugh.)

BERNARD
Did she not cut a figure most wondrously fine
With sword in hand?

GUZMAN
            Aye. If she were mine,
I'd get her to the feast, and slake her thirst—
Though I'd take care to disarm her first.
  (Prepares to leave, halts.)
Madam! I would say a word in this man's behalf.

BERNARD
No, please—

GUZMAN
            Though a veritable monster in the past,
Though a servant-basher. A sausage. A lout.
He's a better man by far with you than without.

JULIE
Thank you, Guzman. I shall bear it in mind.

GUZMAN
Your servant, Madam.
(To BERNARD.) Better luck, this time.
  (Bows and exits regally, if a bit unsteadily.)

BERNARD
My judge, I beg acquittal.

JULIE
Yet which Bernard are you? My executioner?

BERNARD
He is dead. Your lover, born anew.

JULIE
May both a man and a love ever be reborn?

BERNARD
Let me show you proof of a man transformed.
Return with me, home.

JULIE
To what?

BERNARD
Our better lives, within.

JULIE
Our trials, you say, are ended?

BERNARD
Let forgiveness now begin.

(He reaches for her hand. Their eyes meet.)

END OF PLAY

DIRECTOR'S NOTES

DIRECTOR'S NOTES

DIRECTOR'S NOTES

DIRECTOR'S NOTES

DIRECTOR'S NOTES

DIRECTOR'S NOTES